CHRISTIANITY AND OTHER
RELIGIONS

IS VOLUME

146

OF THE

Twentieth Century Encyclopedia of Catholicism

UNDER SECTION

XV

*NON-CHRISTIAN BELIEFS*

IT IS ALSO THE

117TH

VOLUME IN ORDER OF PUBLICATION

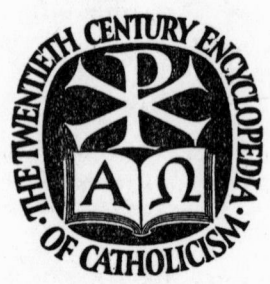

*Edited by* **HENRI DANIEL-ROPS** *of the Académie Française*

# CHRISTIANITY AND OTHER RELIGIONS

## By R. C. ZAEHNER

HAWTHORN BOOKS · PUBLISHERS · *New York*

*First Edition,* April, 1964

NIHIL OBSTAT

Joannes M. T. Barton, S.T.D., L.S.S.

*Censor Deputatus*

IMPRIMATUR

✠ Georgius L. Craven

*Episcopus Sebastopolis, Vicarius Generalis*

Westmonasterii, die XIII JANUARII MCMLXIV

H-9558

# CONTENTS

# INTRODUCTION

After the passing of Pope John XXIII things will never be quite the same again; for, as Louis Fischer has said about another twentieth-century saint, Mahatma Gandhi, who, though not a Christian, yet exhibited on a heroic scale virtues that many Christians mistakenly regard as being peculiar to their own religion: "He did not preach about God and religion; he was a living sermon. He was a good man in a world where few resist the corroding influence of power, wealth, and vanity." Pope John was just this. True, his two Encyclicals introduced a new note of tolerance and warm goodwill not only to those estranged from the Church but also to the Church's enemies that had seldom been heard since the Church emerged from the testing-ground of persecution into the perilous uplands of political power. But it was not the Encyclicals so much that caught the imagination of the world, but the whole rounded personality of this seemingly so ordinary yet wholly extraordinary man who in four and a half years changed not only the whole outlook of the Church but the very image of the Church in the eyes of the non-Catholic world. Where once there had been only suspicion and dislike, there was now sympathy and respect.

The Church has had a very chequered history, and at times it has been very difficult indeed for the uncommitted to see in it the one true Church of Christ. Pope John, alone among the post-Reformation popes, restored that image to something of its pristine brightness, and, thanks to him, there are few indeed today who would still denounce the papacy as Antichrist.

So too in the matter of "error": Pope John was a man of peace who was ready to recognize sincerity and goodwill wherever he might find it, even among those most hostile to the Church and ideologically the furthest removed from her. He was not so much concerned with what separated us from our fellow-Christians and, in a broader context, from all who share in our fallible human nature, as with what we have in common—our humanity and the dignity that, amazing though it may seem, we all possess in the sight of God. He taught us what so many of us, in the evil days of hatred and suspicion that followed the catastrophe of the Reformation, had forgotten, that it is not possible to win souls for Christ unless we not only have, but are seen to have, a charity that is prepared to search out truth in even the most unlikely quarters and to graft it on to the truth we believe we possess in Christ. Thus in our approach to the non-Christian religions we waste our time in pinpointing the differences that separate us since these are obvious enough: rather, we must seek to understand them from within and try to grasp how they too seek to penetrate the mystery of our being and our eternal destiny; for they too have a magnificent heritage of ripe spirituality from which Christians can learn and profit. And it is far more true of the great religions of Asia than it ever was of Pagan Athens that God "left not himself without testimony" (Acts 14. 16).

In the early Christian centuries the Catholic Church rejoiced to build into herself whatever in Paganism she found compatible with and adaptable to the revelation of which she deemed herself to be the depository. Without in any way watering down the message she had received from her divine Founder, she gathered into herself all the riches and all the wisdom that she found scattered throughout the Graeco-Roman world. Since her message had been overwhelmingly rejected by the chosen race to whom it was originally addressed, she had to present it to the Gentiles in thought-forms that they could understand; and so the Gospel was adapted more and more to a Greek view of life, and in the course of time both Plato and Aristotle were "baptized", as it were, into the Catholic Church. The absorption of Greek thought into Christianity was completed in the fourteenth century in the gigantic synthesis of St Thomas Aquinas—fourteen centuries of patient effort which aimed at fitting the Christian message firmly into the frame of the Graeco-Roman philosophical tradition and hallowing that tradition itself under the sign of Christ's Cross.

For historical reasons Christianity in its early centuries made progress mainly in the Roman Empire of which Europe is the heir. What progress it had made in Asia and Africa was largely nullified by the rise of Islam in the seventh century; and it was only in the seventeenth century that the Gospel was again preached in Asia. Indeed it was preached there for the first time in India, China and Japan (except in the case of the St Thomas Christians of southern India who exist to this day). Thus, effectively, there have been only three Christian centuries in Asia as against twenty in Europe. It is, then, scarcely a matter of surprise that so little progress has been made, it is rather a matter of humble satisfaction that there has been any progress at all; for the obstacles have been very great, and the greatest of them have been of our own making.

Certainly, there were obstacles enough to the spread of Christianity in its early days, but the Church was able to triumph over them for she possessed a burning and fearless faith that was strong enough to turn persecution itself into a blessing. "If this counsel or this work be of men," the wise Gamaliel had said, "it will come to nought: but if it be of God, you cannot overthrow it, lest perhaps you be found even to fight against God" (Acts 5. 38–9). The history of the early Church proved that it was of God, and even the might of Rome proved in the long run to be powerless against it. It can, however, be argued that Christianity's conquest of the Roman Empire was the biggest disaster in its history—a disaster the effects of which we are only now beginning to outlive. For the conversion of an Empire inevitably led to the assimilation of a secular spirit into an organism that had hitherto sought its life only in the Holy Spirit that it had received from Christ. This temptation the Lord himself had known—and spurned. As Scripture says: "The devil took him up into a very high mountain and shewed him all the kingdoms of the world and the glory of them, and said to him: All these will I give thee, if falling down, thou wilt adore me. Then Jesus saith to him: Begone, Satan! For it is written: The Lord thy God shalt thou adore, and him only shalt thou serve" (Matt. 4. 8–10). The Tempter was later to offer the same glittering prize to Christ's Bride, the Church, and she could not find it in her to refuse outright. And so it came about that for centuries the Church became inextricably involved in secular politics and, since the Reformation, identified with nation States. Only now does she at last seem to have succeeded in disentangling herself from this deadly embrace.

The Church's first appearance in Asia was thus very different from her humble beginnings in Europe. The Christian missionaries followed on the great voyages of discovery and the imperialist ventures that succeeded them. From the very beginnings, then, the missionaries were regarded as being the henchmen of the imperialist powers. In many cases this was unfair, particularly in the case of the Jesuits whose selfless service in lands utterly strange to them merits nothing but praise. In the eyes of the Asian peoples, however, imperialism and Christianity went together, and conversion all too often meant not only the adoption of a new and alien religion but also the adoption of a new and alien way of life. The converts would thus abandon the ancient cultures that had nurtured them and transform themselves into not very convincing Portuguese, Spaniards, Dutchmen, Englishmen, or Frenchmen as the case might be; and, more scandalous still, the schisms produced by the Reformation were reflected in the Asian converts, their new religion depending on the religion of the particular nation State that was in the process of imposing its will on their native lands. The first image that Asia was to receive of the Church was very different from the image of it that the Roman Empire had witnessed in those early centuries when Christianity neither had nor wished to have the heady experience of power.

The Catholic Church, certainly, was less handicapped than the competing Protestant bodies in that, even after most of Northern Europe had thrown off the Roman obedience, the image of catholicity remained; for it was not easily identified with any one national interest as were the Anglicans, for instance, with England, the Calvinists with Holland, and the Lutherans with Germany. Indeed, the Holy See very often had the wisdom to send priests of a different nationality from that of the imperialist power directly concerned in the newly discovered territories. The conversion of the Americas and later of central and southern Africa followed swiftly on the conquest of these vast areas by the European nations, and the particular brand of Christianity adopted would be that of the conquering race—Catholicism in South America, for instance, and Protestantism in the North. Asia, however, presented a quite different problem: for in Asia the European mariners found ancient civilizations with highly developed cultures immeasurably older than their own—cultures which, because of their immemorial antiquity, could not but despise the brash newcomer with his, to them, unceremonious, uncouth and brutish ways. Moreover, just as the Catholic Church had constituted the spiritual as well as the cultural core of medieval Europe, so did the great Eastern religions constitute the spiritual core of the great Asian civilizations. And so, until very recent times, conversion meant not only a change of religion but also a transference of all the convert's loyalties from the indigenous civilization in which he had his roots to the culture and mores of a seemingly barbarous people hitherto unknown to him. The outward and visible sign of this transformation would be the adoption not only of a Christian name to signify the change of faith but also of a European surname to demonstrate the change of cultural allegiance.

In the Roman Empire the Christian Church developed and grew in spite of and against the Imperial power. In Asia in the seventeenth century she appeared as, and often was, no more than the handmaid of the new, self-confident imperialisms: she came not as a suffering servant but rather as the conqueror's bride. With the decline of Portuguese and Spanish power and the rise of Dutch and British imperialism in the East, however, Catholic missionaries were seen in a rather more favourable light, whereas the Protestants who quickly followed them in the field could not divest themselves of the impalpable but omnipresent odium that was building up against them as the spiritual representatives of the imperialists in the hearts of the outraged peoples. To them Christianity did not appear as a new religion to be judged on its own merits, still less did it appear as "good news" to be accepted with joy; it appeared as the religion of what Mr E. M. Forster has, with his usual accuracy, described as pinko-grey man with all his overweening self-confidence and unsubtle ways.

The imperialist expansion of the European powers in the seventeenth and eighteenth centuries was followed, on the ideological plane, by the intellectual assault by the French Enlightenment on all forms of Christianity and, on the purely material plane, by the Industrial Revolution. The secular age had already begun. Henceforth, in Asian eyes, Europe was now not only the standard-bearer of a divided Christianity which only very few were ever tempted to embrace, but also—and far more significantly—the harbinger of a new and free society which would make an end of priests and kings and the possessor of new and seemingly magical techniques which brought with them prosperity and power. Both of these seemed desirable prizes, and both militated against Christianity; for already in Europe that wily old pupil of the Jesuits, Voltaire, in his attack on established Christianity, was proclaiming the superiority of the Chinese religion to what he considered to be the impossible and irrational superstitions still maintained by the Church he had done so much to discredit. And the irony of the situation was that it was the Jesuits themselves who, in their patient endeavour to understand the Chinese mind from within, had made the first translations of the Chinese Classics available to Europe.

The age of "progress" and humanism had begun, and the Church, which had at long last come to some sort of *modus vivendi* with the Protestant bodies, was regarded merely as an antiquated though still powerful survival from a superstitious past. The conflict between science and religion had begun, and the Christian reaction to the advance of science was all too often both timorous and confused. This surely need never have been so, for the Church, like all religions, concerns herself primarily with eternal values and, in the sphere of our temporal life on earth, with moral values about which science, being concerned with matter and the laws that govern it, can tell us absolutely nothing. In the nineteenth century, however, science and rationalism marched hand in hand, and both of them disliked and despised the Christian Churches and the Catholic Church in particular. This humanist ideology duly made its way into Asia, and it was this aspect of European culture that the young intellectuals of Asia, in many cases waking up from centuries of stagnation, found excitingly new. Europe, apparently, no longer found Christianity relevant: why then should Asia be asked to cast off her own "superstitions" only to accept European superstitions which the Europeans themselves were beginning to ridicule? Could anything be more absurd than this?

The Christian missionaries—and the Protestants were more prominent in this respect than were the Catholics—had perhaps been over-zealous in pointing accusing fingers at the religions among which they worked, too ready to dismiss as mere "idol-worship" practices the inner significance of which they did not begin to understand; for by so doing they started a process that was to lead not to any wholesale conversion but rather to a slow sapping of the religious roots from which the Asian cultures had for centuries grown. The second—secular—wave of European invasion was only to accelerate a process which the missionaries had already set in motion.

Christianity has had some two hundred years in which to adjust itself to the new world created by science and the successive non-Christian ideologies that have accompanied it; but we needed a Pope John to teach us that we would do well to seek out the truth and the idealism that can be found in even the most remote ideologies rather than to condemn outright what we have not first learnt to understand. It is a great pity that the Catholic Church remains an overwhelmingly European organization with an overwhelmingly European look; but it is nonetheless fortunate that, being on the spot in Europe, she has been able to counter the rationalist attack in the place of its unleashing. The Eastern religions have not had this advantage, and the assault on their traditional values has therefore been the more violent. China, indeed, is an extreme case, but it is an object-lesson on what may happen elsewhere in Asia; for of all the civilizations of Asia the Chinese was the most ancient and stable, having an unbroken history stretching right back to legendary times. Of all the empires of the world it was the most ancient and it had outlasted them all, yet when the time came it succumbed most easily to the new Western ideas first of republican demo- cracy and secondly of Communism. Some four thousand years of unbroken history were swept away in less than half a century. What had for centuries been the State "religion" of China— Confucianism—has been totally dismantled; and the other two "religions" of China—Taoism and Buddhism—are probably in a no better case. How do things stand with the other religions?

Before we can answer this question at all, however, we need to study the religious map of the world and to consider the nature of the religions that still claim the allegiance of man. The first fact that strikes us is that all the religions that survive today originate in Asia—Judaism and Christianity in Palestine, Islam in Arabia, Hinduism and Buddhism in India, Confucianism and Taoism in China. Of these four can be considered as national religions—Judaism being the religion of the Jewish people, Hinduism being that of the Indian people, whereas Confucian- ism and Taoism are so peculiarly Chinese that they have exer- cised little influence outside the Chinese Empire except in Korea and Japan.

Apart from Christianity only two of these religions are tradi- tionally missionary religions—Islam and Buddhism, the one originating among a Semitic people, the other in India. If we disregard Confucianism and Taoism for our present purposes as being rather systems of thought than religions in the strict sense of the word, it will be seen that the religions which have survived originate, all of them, either in Israel or in India; and the develop- ment of each religious stream bears a curious resemblance to the other. In each case we start with the national religion of a people, and from this another religion stems—rejected by the people as a whole from which it has sprung but disseminated and enthusiastically welcomed by other peoples with quite other traditions. Out of Judaism, as we all know, Christianity was born: out of Hinduism came Buddhism. But the resemblance does not stop here, for in each case some six hundred years after

the founding of the daughter religion another religion has sprung
up, similar in type but distinct—Islam on the Semitic side,
Mahāyāna Buddhism on the Indian. In each case again the older
religion rejects the new: Christianity rejects Islam, primitive
Buddhism rejects the Mahāyāna.

This parallelism between the Near Eastern and Indian religious streams is, however, all in form, not in content; for so
different are these two *types* of religion that one sometimes wonders whether they are concerned with the same problem, whether
indeed they are talking about the same thing. And it is for this
reason that the average Westerner has the greatest difficulty in
understanding the religions of Indian origin; he just doesn't
understand what they are *about*. With Islam things are very
different; for Islam derives from the same Judaic root as Christianity, and it is talking about the same things in the same way.
We differ from the Muslims as we differ from the Jews, but one
thing at least we have in common, and that is that we all believe
in One God who is both just and merciful, omnipotent and
omniscient, and who acts in history. The cardinal doctrines of
Christianity, however, the Incarnation and the Holy Trinity, are
totally unacceptable to the strict monotheism of the Jews and
Muslims, but they are precisely the doctrines that enable us to
enter into fruitful dialogue with the Indian religions, as we shall
see.

Again, for all three Semitic religions God is a transcendent
reality who is vitally concerned with the doings of men in this
world: he commands and he prohibits; he makes his will known
through the prophets whom he himself chooses, and he demands
of man that he obey. The essence of both Judaism and Islam is
prophecy. For the Jews God promulgated his Law through the
first and greatest of the Jewish prophets, Moses, and supplemented it through the later prophets. All this the Muslims accept.
They accept too Jesus as Messias, not indeed as the Son of God
and Son of Man, but as the last and greatest of the Jewish prophets and the direct precursor of the Arabian prophet, Muhammad. Though there is a deep cleavage between us on the nature
and mission of Jesus Christ, we are at least united in worshipping

the One God whom *we* call the Father, *they* "the Merciful, the Compassionate, Lord of the Day of Judgement". We differ on matters that to us as Christians are of crucial importance, but we agree on the basic issue, namely, that God is a righteous though merciful judge, that we are responsible before him, and that we will be rewarded or punished in another existence for what of good or evil we have done on earth. When we differ, moreover, we know what we are differing about, and we can for this reason respect the opposing point of view and, if we feel inclined, seek to bring the other party over to our way of thinking: we will not be talking at cross purposes because we start from the same premisses.

With Indian and, to a lesser extent, Chinese religion things are very different. The premisses from which we start are *not* the same. For the Hindu, obedience to the will of God is not the essential prerequisite of religion; indeed it can be said that it has little relevance for him whether there is one God or many or even if there is none at all. Salvation, for him, does not mean primarily salvation from sin, but salvation or rather liberation from our human condition as such. Buddhism too, which is more coherent than Hinduism, is even more emphatic on this point. From the Western point of view southern (Theravāda) Buddhism, which is usually considered to be nearer to the Buddha's own teaching, is an atheistic creed. It does not admit the existence of a God who creates, sustains and guides the universe. Like the Pagan religions of Greece and Rome it *does* admit the existence of "gods", but these gods, like men, are subject to birth and ultimately to death. They may live for countless eons, but a day will come when they too will die only to be born again in another mode of existence. And this brings us to another fundamental cleavage between the two groups of religions—reincarnation or the transmigration of souls.

In the Semitic tradition man is born once and for all: he lives one life only and is rewarded or punished for what he does with himself in that one life. In Indian religion things are very different. Time is not a simple affair with a beginning, a middle, and an end as it is for the Semites: it is cyclic, that is to say, it moves in ever recurring cycles from eternity without beginning to eternity without end. Periods of activity alternate with periods of rest; but there is no *final* rest, for the cosmic machine goes on and on, and there is no end to the process. Man is inexorably caught up in this machine and, unless he is shown the way, he can never escape. This, for the Buddha, was an appalling prospect—so appalling indeed that he analysed human existence itself as being nothing more nor less than "pain". For him "pain" and "transient" are interchangeable words: what is transient is necessarily painful since it must come to an end. Life itself is, then, an evil from which escape must be sought. Were the belief in transmigration not so deeply rooted in India as to be accepted as a self-evident fact of existence, Indian religion might have developed on very different lines—on the same lines as it developed in China for instance. For better or for worse, however, transmigration is the unchallenged premiss from which all Indian religion, at least from the seventh century B.C., starts; and the prospect of eternal life in *this* sense seemed too appalling to be borne. Hence Indian religion concerned itself not with the existence of God or with any service we might owe him but with the practical ways and means of escaping from this eternal round of ever-recurring birth and death, rebirth and re-death.

Given this pessimistic view of human life Indian religion was bound to develop on mystical lines. There are many types of mysticism, and I have attempted to analyse them in two earlier works, *Mysticism Sacred and Profane* and *Hindu and Muslim Mysticism*. Since, however, there is much confusion in this matter, I must restate my conclusions here.

There is, of course, a great mystical tradition within the Catholic Church starting with St John the Evangelist and culminating in St John of the Cross. In Catholic mysticism the essential element is love: it is the direct experience here and now of God's burning love for the soul and of the answering love that God awakens in that soul. The soul is conscious all the time that it is utterly unworthy of this love, and it knows that it cannot attain to union with God until the last vestige of selfishness and sin has been burnt out of it by the fire of the Holy Spirit. The state of union when it is at last achieved is so close and intimate and our human condition has been so transformed that we may literally speak of the "deification" of the soul. This "deification" is the corollary of the Incarnation: God becomes Man that man may become God. This tremendous fact should not surprise us, for every time we go to Mass we repeat these wonderful words: *Da nobis per hujus aquae et vini mysterium, ejus divinitatis esse consortes, qui humanitatis nostrae fieri dignatus est particeps, Jesus Christus, Filius tuus, Dominus noster* ("Through the mystery of this water and wine, grant us that we may be sharers in the divinity of him who condescended to share in our humanity, Jesus Christ, your Son, our Lord"). Christ became Man that we might become God. Every time we go to Holy Communion, so long as we are in a state of grace, we share in God's own godhead—we are "deified". We are not conscious of it: the mystic is. Therein lies the difference.

Love is and must be the essential element in Catholic mysticism, for we are taught that God *is* love. There are types of mysticism, however, in which love plays no part as, for example, in primitive Buddhism. What all religious mystics, however, agree about is that all trace of self must be obliterated if there is to be a mystical experience of any sort. But, if there is to be union with God, does this not imply that there must be a "self" with which God can unite? The question is a legitimate one, and the answer is "Yes". Two "selves" in fact must be distinguished in man, the "selfish" one which psychologists call the "ego" and a higher one which psychologists of the Jungian school, following Hindu precedent, call simply the "self". The distinction between these two selves is much more rigorously emphasized in the mysticism of India than it is in the Western Catholic tradition, and it is only recently that this distinction has been given its due weight by a Catholic mystic. I am speaking of one who seems to me to be the most remarkable mystic of our times, the American Cistercian monk, Thomas Merton. On this all-important subject he writes (and this passage should be read again and again by the reader who wishes to understand the sequel):

Contemplation is not and cannot be a function of this external self. There is an irreducible opposition between the deep transcendent self that awakens only in contemplation, and the superficial, external self which we commonly identify with the first person singular. We must remember that this superficial "I" is not our real self. It is our "individuality" and our "empirical self" but it is not truly the hidden and mysterious person in whom we subsist before the eyes of God. The "I" that works in the world, thinks about itself, observes its own reactions and talks about itself is not the true "I" that has been united to God in Christ. It is at best the vesture, the mask, the disguise of that mysterious and unknown "self" whom most of us never discover until we are dead. Our external, superficial self is not eternal, not spiritual. Far from it. This self is doomed to disappear as completely as smoke from a chimney. It is utterly frail and evanescent. Contemplation is precisely the awareness that this "I" is really "not I" and the awakening of the unknown "I" that is beyond observation and reflection and is incapable of commenting upon itself. It cannot even say "I" with the assurance and the impertinence of the other one, for its very nature is to be hidden, unnamed, unidentified in the society where men talk about themselves and about one another. In such a world the true "I" remains both inarticulate and invisible, because it has altogether too much to say—not one word of which is about itself (*New Seeds of Contemplation*, pp. 5-6).

Now it is this "deep, transcendent self" that is the object of the quest of the Hindu and, I believe, the Buddhist too: it is the image of God in man and the fact that "most of us never discover it until we are dead" is due to original and actual sin. In the words of Thomas Merton "to reach one's 'real self' one must, in fact, be delivered by grace, virtue and asceticism, from that illusory and false 'self' whom we have created by our habits of selfishness and by our constant flights from reality. In order to find God, Whom we can only find in and through the depths of our own soul, *we must therefore first find ourselves*" (*The New Man*, p. 44). In other words, we cannot begin to know and love God before we have discovered our true self.

The habitat of this true self is beyond space and time in an eternal "now" as the fourteenth-century German mystic,

Eckhart, never tired of pointing out: it knows neither past nor future—it simply *is*. To know it is to know one cannot die. This sense of timelessness, however, which is much less stressed in Catholic mysticism than it is in Hinduism and Buddhism, does not necessarily bring with it any awareness of God as a Person distinct from oneself. It is, however, accompanied by a sense of immortality because what exists outside time can clearly never die. It is frequently, though not always, accompanied by an experience of absolute oneness, which is felt to be an ultimate, a *summum bonum*, beyond which, it seems, it is impossible to proceed. In this experience there is no knowledge of God as distinct from the eternal, timeless "true self", and there being no knowledge of him, there is no love of him. This is the mysticism of the "self" as experienced without concious reference to God.

There is, however, a third type of mysticism usually called "nature mysticism" in which the barrier between the "self" and the "not-self", the experiencing subject and the objective world seems to vanish, and all is seen as one and one as all. This type of mysticism can be and is experienced by people of all religions and by people who have no religion at all. Moreover, it has nothing to do with morality, and we shall be hearing a lot about transcending good and evil in the sequel. For the present, however, we must be content to emphasize the fact that there are three types of mysticism that can and must be distinguished from one another. Let us repeat what these are.

Starting with what appears to be the lowest, we have *first* nature mysticism in which all distinction between subject and object appears to vanish away. Many purely secular writers have described this, and we can do worse than quote Tennyson since his description of it is one of the best and the most succinct:

A kind of waking trance [he writes]—this for lack of a better word—I have frequently had, quite up from boyhood, when I have been all alone. This has come upon me through repeating my own name to myself silently, till all at once, as it were out of the intensity of the consciousness of individuality, individuality itself seemed to dissolve and fade away into boundless being, and this not a confused state but the clearest, the surest of the surest, utterly

beyond words—where death was an almost laughable impossibility
—the loss of personality (if so it were) seeming no extinction, but
the only true life. I am ashamed of my feeble description. Have I not
said the state is utterly beyond words? (Quoted in R. C. Zaehner,
*Mysticism Sacred and Profane*, pp. 36–7).

Much that we will meet with in the Indian and Chinese sacred
books will remind us of this passage. The core of the experience
is that "individuality itself seems to dissolve and fade away", and
this brings joy and peace.

The *second* type of mysticism is the experience of absolute
oneness, what the *Sāṁkhya-Yoga* system of philosophy in India
calls "isolation". This is not peculiar to India but has been more
intensively cultivated there than anywhere else. It is sometimes
interpreted as meaning no more than the isolation of one individual "self" in its own deep essence—which is not inconsistent
with Catholic theology—or it is interpreted as meaning that the
soul in its inmost essence is *identical* with the essence of God—
and this, if left wholly unqualified, is.

The *third* type, with which Catholics will be more familiar, is
the mysticism of the love of God. God takes the initiative: it is
he who loves the soul first, and by the soul is meant, as Thomas
Merton has made so admirably clear, not the empirical "ego"
but the "true, transcendent self": it is the love of God for his
own image in the human soul, it is the love of the Father for the
Son who, as Eckhart says, must be conceived in the soul just as
he was conceived in the body of the Blessed Virgin. It is the love
of Person for person in which the two must ultimately be made
one just as man and woman are made one in the sacrament of
marriage.

These remarks on mysticism in general were necessary since
Indian religion, in all its phases, is mystical through and through,
and much of this little book will necessarily be taken up with the
Indian experience of the divine.

We earlier made a distinction between "prophetic" and
"mystical" religion. "Prophetic" religion teaches how God wills
that we should act in this world: mystical religion, on the other
hand, brings us experience of another world that transcends this

one, for it transcends space and time by which this world is conditioned. Martha is the figure of the prophetic type of religion, Mary of the mystical. More generally, the two types of religion could be described as religions of action and religions of contemplation, or, if you like, this-worldly religions and other-worldly religions. Judaism, Islam, Protestantism, and Confucianism are predominantly this-worldly religions, stressing as they do the need for righteous conduct here on earth; Hinduism, Theravāda Buddhism, and Taoism are predominantly other-worldly religions, insisting all the time that there is a timeless reality beyond this world which it is in man's power to reach. In between the extremes stand Mahāyāna Buddhism, Neo-Confucianism, the reformed Hinduism of Gandhi and Tagore, and the Catholic Church. This book sets out to outline the religions of India and China in their historical development, to consider the very special case of Islam, and to correlate our findings, so far as we can, with the teachings of the Catholic Church.

# CHAPTER I

# INDIA

From the unreal lead me to the real!
From darkness lead me to light!
From death lead me to immortality!
(*Brihadāranyaka* Upanishad, 1.3.28)

Each of the great religions possesses a sacred literature. The
sacred book of the Hindus is known as the *Veda*, meaning
"knowledge". This is divided into three parts: (i) the *Saṁhitās* or
"collections" of hymns and sacred formulas, (ii) the *Brāhmanas*
which deal mainly with the sacrificial ritual, and (iii) the *Upanishads*. Though lip-service is still paid to the *Saṁhitās* and
*Brāhmanas*, it is the Upanishads that constitute the core of the
Veda and the source from which later Hinduism flows. The whole
Veda is believed to be uncreated: it is the Word spoken by the
Absolute in eternity and "heard" and memorized by sages of
immemorial antiquity; but it is the Upanishads which contain
its essence.

The Veda does not in the least resemble our Bible. It is not an
account of God's dealings with man in history; rather it is a
gradual revelation of the being of God and of man. Man is seen
groping in the dark at first but becoming ever more sure in his
quest for the Eternal, the Real, and the Light, both in himself
and in the world that surrounds him. He speculates on how the
world began and sees only an unfathomable mystery:

Then neither Being nor Not-Being existed, neither atmosphere,
nor the firmament, nor what is above it. What did it encompass?
Where? In whose protection? What was water, the deep, unfathomable?
Neither death nor immortality was there then, no sign of night or

day. The One breathed windless by its own power. Nought else but this existed then.

In the beginning was darkness swathed in darkness: all this was but unmanifested water. Whatever was, that One, coming into being, hidden by the void, was generated by the power of heat.

In the beginning desire which was the first seed of mind over-covered it. Wise seers, searching in their hearts, found the bond of Being in Not-Being.

Their cord was extended athwart. Was there anything above or anything below? Givers of seed there were, and powers; beneath was energy and above impulse.

Who knows truly? Who can here declare whence it was born, whence is this emanation. By the emanation of this the gods [came into existence] only later. Who knows whence it has arisen?

Whence this emanation has arisen, whether [God] created it or whether he did not, only he who is its overseer in highest heaven knows. [He only knows] or perhaps he does not know (*Rig-Veda*, 10. 129).

## THE UPANISHADS

The quest for the Absolute has begun, but the riddle as yet remains unsolved. What is Brahman? What is the Absolute? What is the Self of all things and of the individual human being? These are the questions the ancient sages of India were asking. The early answers did not satisfy them. Some said Brahman was food, that is, matter; others the breath of life; yet others the ether or space which, since it pervades everything, might well be the ground of all things. Or again would it not be better to say of it no more than "No! No!" since once you define it you limit it, and, whatever it is, it is certainly not limited or circumscribed. Or again, if living creatures can be described as "real" even though they are subject to change and pass away, Brahman which is the true "self" of all things must be the "real of the real" (*Brihadāranyaka* Upanishad 2. 3. 6). It is the "Inner Controller", the "inmost Self", the warp and woof of all things, the "unseen seer, the unheard hearer, the unthought thinker, the ununderstood understander" (*ibid.*, 3. 8. 11), other than the world but controlling it from within. In short Brahman is both eternal Being and the source of all that comes to be and passes away—and it is also the inmost self in the heart of man. This famous identification of the eternal essence of man with the changeless godhead that indwells and controls the whole universe was made at a very early date and is most beautifully formulated in the *Chāndogya* Upanishad 3. 14:

> One should venerate Brahman as the True. . . . One should venerate the Self who consists of mind, whose body is breath, whose form is light, whose self is space, who changes his form at will, whose thought is swift, whose conception is true, whose resolve is true, in whom are all scents and tastes, who holds sway over all the points of the compass, who encompasses all this [world], who does not speak and has no care—like a grain of rice or a barley corn or a grain of millet or the kernel of a grain of millet is this Person within the self, golden like a smokeless flame—greater than the sky, greater than space, greater than this earth, greater than all existing things. He is the Self of life, he is my own self. This my self within the heart is that Brahman. When I depart from hence I shall merge into it.

Here the Upanishad describes the nature of God and the soul and their relationship to one another almost exactly as Thomas Merton does. God indwells the soul in so intimate a manner that it is possible to speak of him as the Self of all selves. These selves are not the "empirical" selves or egos that operate in space and time but the "transcendent" selves of which Thomas Merton speaks so eloquently. At death their union with God is so close that it is possible to speak of them merging into him. "An ocean, a seer alone without duality, becomes he whose world is Brahman. . . . This is a man's highest path. This is his highest achievement. This is his highest world. This is his highest bliss" (*Brihadāranyaka* Upanishad 4. 3. 32).

The mystic's union with God is so close, so ineffably intimate that it is possible even for so good a Catholic as Thomas Merton to speak of "identity". "This inmost self", he writes, "is beyond the kind of experience which says 'I want', 'I love', 'I know', 'I feel'. It has its own way of knowing, loving and experiencing which is a divine way and not a human one, a way of identity, of union, of 'espousal', in which there is no longer a separate psychological individuality drawing all good and all truth towards itself, and thus loving and knowing for itself. Lover and Beloved are 'one spirit'" (*New Seeds of Contemplation*, p. 219).

Does this mean that our true "self" is identical with God in all respects? According to Merton "No", for he also says: "In order to find God, Whom we can only find in and through the depths of our own soul, we must . . . first find ourselves" (*The New Man*, p. 44). He does not, however, discuss the important question of whether one can find one's true self without later finding God. In Hinduism this question was to assume great importance and was to cause endless controversy.

According to the major trend of the Upanishads the Self of the cosmos and the "Inner Self" of man are identical: both are God in his timeless essence. The "transcendent self" of the individual, however, is distinct from God but merges into him at death. God, however, is also creator and sustainer of the universe and as such is entitled to worship. In a state of ecstasy it is no longer possible to speak or think in terms of time: one is conscious of an unfractionable unity, and all disappears except the One. How should this be interpreted philosophically? One school of thought, the *Sāṁkhya-Yoga*, maintained that the experience of absolute oneness meant no more than that the soul had reached its own ontological centre; another, the non-dualist Vedānta, on the other hand, maintained that it had realized its own identity with the ultimate ground of the universe and that all else, including the creator God himself, was no more than appearance or illusion.

And here an important distinction must be made. It does not occur to Thomas Merton any more than it did to St John of the Cross that mystical union could be possible without love. If there is union at all, then there must originally have been two poles to the resulting unity. There is, however, a type of mystical experience in which there is no question of union but only of realizing an absolute oneness which is the core of one's own being. Is this a stage *beyond* the union of which Thomas Merton speaks, or is it merely a preparatory stage in which the mystic does no more than realize the oneness of his own individual soul? To this the non-dualist Vedāntin would reply that since, according to a text we must now cite, nothing at all exists except the One, God himself must be an appearance of reality only, and that what the soul experiences as union with him is only the last stage in which he is still not free from the world of appearance and which precedes his experience of the ultimate truth—and that is that he actually is the One truly existent Being. The text (*Māndūkya* Upanishad 7) describes this seemingly ultimate state of oneness in the following terms:

> It has cognizance neither of what is inside nor of what is outside nor of both together; it is not a mass of wisdom, it is not wise nor yet unwise. It is unseen; there can be no commerce with it; it is impalpable, has no characteristics, unthinkable; it cannot be designated. Its essence is its firm conviction of the oneness of itself; it causes the phenomenal world to cease; it is tranquil and mild, devoid of duality. Such do they consider this fourth to be. He is the Self; he it is who should be known.

And this "Self", as is here explicitly stated, is Brahman, all else being mere appearance. If this is literally true, then, God himself becomes unreal and therefore irrelevant. This, to us, disquieting discovery the Hindus of the classical period took in their stride, for in the last stage of the life of the three higher castes when a man renounced all things and retired into the desert or jungle to achieve "liberation" from this world of space and time, he was explicitly told that he should give up all religious practices since, if he had indeed realized himself as the One without a second, there would be singularly little point in paying homage to a God who was no more than an appearance of himself. This, however, was only one among many interpretations of the experience.

The Sāṁkhya-Yoga world-picture was quite different. For them the world was neatly divided between what they call *purushas* and *prakriti*. The *purushas* are eternal, "transcendent" souls whose real being is outside time; *prakriti* is Nature, that is, the phenomenal world including mind and what we in the West call "soul" and they call *buddhi*, the faculty through which we know and will. For reasons that remain unexplained the two become inextricably mixed and the result of this fusion is a human being. The mixture, however, is unnatural, and man's goal is simply to extricate his eternal soul from the psycho-physical frame with which it is normally identified. There is a God of sorts, but he is not the creator of the universe though he exercises a general supervision over it. He is a transcendent soul or "self" like all the other souls but, unlike them, he alone has never become entangled in matter. One of the ways of realizing the "oneness" and "isolation" of one's own soul is to contemplate God in *his* eternal isolation. "Liberation", however, means no more than the realization of the utter simplicity of one's own soul: there is no question of union with God or of love for him. Which is the correct interpretation of the experience?

The *Bhagavad-Gītā* which is the best loved of the Hindu scriptures gives the answer to this question, but before we go on to describe the religious revolution occasioned by this remarkable book, a word must be said about the Buddhists and how they interpreted mystical experience.

### THE RISE OF BUDDHISM

The Upanishads are treatises about God and the soul, about "liberation" and how it is to be interpreted. Primitive Buddhism, on the other hand, is thoroughly empirical; it is not interested in metaphysics and speculation, but it *is* interested in showing man the way out of his human condition into that state in which, as Tennyson said, "death is an almost laughable impossibility". This state is called *nirvāna* which literally means the "blowing out" of a flame. In this state there is neither birth nor death nor time nor discursive thought; it is painless and pure, the cessation of all becoming. There is no question of union with Brahman—indeed this idea is ridiculed—nor of communion with any other being; nor is there any question of love, for love itself, like its opposite, hate, is condemned along with all the passions and all the other pairs of opposites. As in other mystical traditions the Buddha insists on a complete detachment from all things, for

only by turning one's back on the temporal can one win through
to the eternal. Primitive Buddhism does not attempt to interpret the experience of eternity as the Hindu philosophical schools do; rather
the Buddha is described as a physician of the human soul. He
strongly disapproved of metaphysics; and all this endless dis-
cussion on what liberation really is he compares to a physician
and a man wounded by an arrow. If a man wounded by an
arrow, he says, were to come to you for help, would you ask him
first who had shot the arrow or would you remove the arrow
and dress the wound? Obviously you would do the latter. Well
then, once a Buddha (meaning literally an "awakened one") has
diagnosed that the whole world is in pain because it is transient
and can find no enduring peace anywhere, he will set about
devising a remedy for it—he will get down to the practical business of showing individual men the way by which *nirvāna* can be
reached. At his own "enlightenment" he had experienced the
ineffable bliss of *nirvāna*, and it was for him to help others across
the stream of transient existence on to the further shore which is
abiding bliss.

Here there is a dichotomy between the Buddha's theory and
practice which the Buddhists never really solved. The Buddha
analysed a human being into five *samskāras* or component parts:
body, feeling, senses, impulses (greed, hate, love, wisdom, etc.)
and consciousness. The combination of these is usually considered to constitute a "self"—what Thomas Merton and others
have called the "empirical" self. According to the Buddhists this
is quite false: none of these nor the combination of them constitutes a self. Body, mind and psyche are constantly changing and
there is no basis in a human being which constitutes a self:
everything in this world is devoid of essence, everything is in
flux. If this is really so, then one wonders why the Buddha should
have considered the saving of such insubstantial creatures so
immensely worthwhile. Time and again his compassion for them
is stressed; but why, one cannot help asking, did one who had
seen the whole world as void of substance, who had detached
himself completely from it, and who had entered into an eternal

state of being, still concern himself with composite and impermanent creatures who were not the same person for two minutes on
end ? There seems to be no answer to this question, unless we are
prepared to accept the theory that the Buddha did admit the
existence of a transcendent self rather on the lines of the
Sāṁkhya-Yoga. Scholars have been singularly reluctant to
admit this, and this seems strange, for there is a whole series of
passages in the early Buddhist Canon in which the Buddha's
disciples are told to make the "self" their refuge and in which
this "self" is said to have achieved *nirvāna*. This state, it may be
said in passing, is also called *brahma-bhūta*, "become Brahman",
but for the Buddhist Brahman is not a cosmic principle but
simply the soul's realization of itself as having an eternal and
timeless dimension.

The Buddhists agree with the Upanishads that an eternal mode
of existence must be the goal towards which man should strive,
but whereas the Hindus argue about how this form of existence
is to be defined and at first say very little about how it is to be
*reached*, the Buddhists care little about definitions but are deeply
interested in the *way* to get there.

On his enlightenment the Buddha claimed to have seen things
as they really are, and this vision he translated into his famous
Four Noble Truths.

What [he asks] is the Noble Truth of Ill? Birth is Ill, old age is
Ill, sickness is Ill, death is Ill, likewise sorrow and grief, woe, lamen-
tation over Ill, and despair. To be conjoined with things we dislike,
to be separated from things we like—that too is Ill. Not to get what
one wants—that too is Ill. In a word this fivefold mass which is based
on grasping [the body]—that too is Ill.

Now this, monks, is the Noble Truth about the origin of Ill. It is
that craving which leads to rebirth, accompanied by delight and
greed, seeking its pleasure now here, now there, namely the craving
for pleasure, the craving for transient existence, the craving for
transient existence to come to an end.

And this, monks, is the Noble Truth concerning the stopping of
Ill. It is to put a complete stop to this craving by passionlessness, to
abandon it, to have done with it, to be liberated from it, to be
independent of it.

And this, monks, is the Noble Truth concerning the path that leads to the stopping of Ill. It is the Noble Eightfold Path, namely, right views, right resolve, right speech, right action, right livelihood, right effort, right mindfulness, right concentration. (*Samyutta Nikāya*, v. 421).

The goal of both Hinduism and Buddhism is the same, namely, the liberation of the timeless element in man from all that has its being in space and time—the liberation of the transcendent self from the empirical one; but, according to the Buddhists, this can only be attained by a combination of a strictly ethical life with controlled meditation and concentration. It was, however, by no means expected that all men were ready for liberation in this life—millions more lives might be required. All men, however, had to observe these basic commandments: you must not kill any living thing; you must not take what has not been given to you; you must not violate chastity; you must not lie; you must not slander or use harsh or frivolous language. These prohibitions correspond almost exactly to the second half of the Ten Commandments—the minimum restraints required of man in his relationship with his fellow-man. What, however, is entirely lacking in the Buddhist "law" is any reference to man's duty to God. And the reason is obvious: the Buddha did not believe in the existence of a personal God who is the moral governor of the world. Even were the existence of such a Being to be proved, he would still be irrelevant to man, for man is the master of his own destiny; he has it in him to win through to an eternal mode of existence in which he is forever free from sorrow and from all that comes to be and passes away. And once again we are amazed that the Buddha, the preacher of a complete detachment from all things worldly, should at the same time speak of compassion, selfless giving, and the refusal to harm any living thing as the highest virtues. Such respect for physical life seems strange in one who saw in it only pain and "Ill" and whose ideal was the passionless peace and timeless bliss of *nirvāna* which also means the extinction of life as we know it.

Buddhism asserts that man's salvation lies firmly in his own hands, and that the Buddha and the *dharma* ("religion, way of life") which he proclaimed can only point the way. It is the individual man himself who is ultimately responsible for his own salvation.

## THE RISE OF THEISM

Hinduism, meanwhile, was beginning to take another course: already in the later Upanishads we find a new trend developing. The supreme "Self" is now seen not only as a static principle that lies concealed beneath all change and which indwells the human soul: it is also a personal God who chooses and operates by grace. Thus we read that by the *grace* of the Creator one can behold the greatness of the supreme Self (*Katha* Upanishad 2.20) who is at the same time God (*ibid.*, 2.12). "This Self is not to be found by instruction, Not by intellect, nor yet by much lore heard; He can be found only by such as he chooses, To such does he reveal his bodily form" (*ibid.*, 2.23).

The supreme Self is thus seen to be God—not just one god among many as in the earlier literature, but the Supreme Being, the "Inner Self" and "Inner Controller". He is not merely an eternal mode of being but a responsible agent who chooses, ordains and disposes.

In the earlier parts of the Veda a great variety of gods are worshipped. Some of them represent natural phenomena while others are personifications of moral principles—Mitra, the "contract", Varuna, according to some modern scholars, the "oath" and so on. Only two of the ancient gods, however, achieved complete pre-eminence and came to be regarded as "God", the supreme ruler of the universe, very much on the lines that Zeus attained to this supreme position in ancient Greece. These two were Rudra-Shiva and Vishnu.

The rather late and certainly post-Buddhistic Upanishad, the *Shvetāshvatara*, is dedicated to the God Rudra-Shiva. He is hailed as the supreme Brahman and the highest Self—the supreme Lord who is master of the eternal as well as the transient, the imperishable as well as the perishable (1.10): he is "the One —they admit of no second—who rules all the worlds with his ruling powers. Over against his creatures he stands. He, the Protector, creates all things and welds them together at the end of time" (3.2). To know God means to become immortal: "whoso knows him with heart and mind as dwelling in the heart becomes immortal" (4.20). Liberation, then, consists in *knowing* God as "dwelling in the heart". It is also described as having access to Brahman (6.10), as being merged in Brahman (1.7), both of which mean here participation in eternal being, or it is described as "isolation" as in the Sāṁkhya-Yoga. The relationship between "self", Brahman, and God is, however, best formulated in 2.14–15.

> Even as a mirror smeared over with dirt shines brightly once it has been cleaned,
> So does he who dwells in the body (the soul in the Western sense), once it has beheld its own "self" as it really is, become one, its goal achieved and free from sorrow.
> When a man [thus] integrated beholds Brahman as it really is by means of his "self" as it really is, as with a lamp,
> Then does he know the unborn, pure God who transcends all things as they really are, and [knowing him] is released from all fetters.

In this passage there are three stages in the process of "liberation". First there is the integration of the total personality around the "transcendent self"; next, this self throws its light on Brahman as with a lamp—it illumines the whole sphere of eternal and timeless existence that had previously been hidden from it. With both time and eternity laid bare before its eyes it comes to "know" God who transcends eternity as he transcends time. "Knowing" in this passage as elsewhere is not at all what we normally understand by that word: it is a flash of intuition sometimes compared to a flash of lightning, a sudden illumination of the contemplative intellect, as Christian mystics would say.

Christian mystics, however, regard the mystical union as being the joint affair of the contemplative intellect and the will. God is not only "comprehended" by the intellect, he is also loved in the will; and perfect union means that the human will is completely "conformed" to the will of God. It is not enough to experience God as timeless Being, we must also unite with him

in his loving will since he has placed us in this world for a purpose—and that purpose is very much more than the salvation of
your soul or mine, it is the redemption of the whole human race.
This idea we will rarely find in Hindu mysticism which tends to
remain strictly on the plane of personal salvation.

In the Upanishads we hear almost nothing about the love of
God for man: it is only in the *Bhagavad-Gītā* that we begin to be
told about it.

## THE BHAGAVAD-GĪTĀ

The *Bhagavad-Gītā* is later than the Upanishads and forms
part of the *Mahābhārata*, India's Great Epic. It is a dialogue
between Krishna and Arjuna. Krishna is the incarnation of the
great God, Vishnu; Arjuna is one of the five Pāndava brothers
who are about to go to war with their cousins, the Kauravas,
who have usurped their kingdom. The opposing ranks are drawn
up on either side, but at the last moment Arjuna's heart fails him
at the thought of the fratricidal slaughter in which he must share.
Krishna, however, is determined that the war shall be fought
to the finish and in the *Gītā* he not only convinces Arjuna
that the struggle must go on, he also reveals to him much concerning the "self", Brahman, and the incarnate God that he
himself is.

First he tells him that the soul not only lives again in future
incarnations; it is also a timeless essence which of its nature can
in no way be affected by the life or death of the body: nobody
slays and nobody is slain. This leads him on to discuss ways and
means by which the soul can achieve liberation here and now in
this life, and what liberation means. The terminology of the
*Gītā* is largely Buddhistic and it can therefore be seen as a theistic counter-blast to Buddhist propaganda. If liberation in
*nirvāna*, if "becoming Brahman" is the highest point that man
can reach, what relevance can God have? And Krishna, it must
be remembered, is God incarnate. Thus he returns to the subject
four times and each time there is a shift of emphasis. The first
passage (chapter ii) is couched largely in Buddhistic terms, and

the complete changelessness and timelessness of the state of *nirvāna* is strongly emphasized: it is the "state of Brahman", and God has no relevance to it. He is only mentioned once and then only as an object of contemplation: from the actual state of liberation he is wholly absent.

The same position is further elaborated in chapter v but with special reference to Brahman, "the flawless, whose nature is one and the same". The mind of the liberated man "abides in this sameness" and therefore "in Brahman". "His self integrated by the Yoga of Brahman he attains to imperishable bliss. . . . His joy within, his light within, become Brahman, he goes to the *nirvāna* of Brahman." Here again the emphasis is all on a total detachment from all that is not Brahman: only so can one "become Brahman" and enter the *"nirvāna* of Brahman". The term *brahma-bhūta*, "become Brahman", is, as we have seen, borrowed from Buddhism—and the compound *brahma-nirvāna*, the *"nirvāna* of Brahman", is used no less than three times in this passage. Throughout the whole passage God is not so much as mentioned: man has it in himself to realize here and now what the medieval mystics called the apex of his soul which is changeless, static, still, and absolutely detached from all that is conditioned by space and time. This is Brahman, and this is *nirvāna* —perfect bliss and timeless peace; and all this man can discover in himself if he will but resort to the "Yoga of Brahman". This would appear to be man's final beatitude, but the last stanza introduces a new note. The liberated man, Krishna says, "recognizing *me* as the object of sacrifice and mortification, as the great Lord of the whole universe, as the friend of all beings, attains to peace". Here for the first time Krishna hints that liberation from the bonds of matter, essential though it may be for the enjoyment of any purely spiritual life, is perhaps not in itself man's ultimate goal.

In chapter v all the emphasis had been on Brahman: in chapter vi, which largely recapitulates it, it is all on *ātman*, the "true, transcendent self" of Thomas Merton which he also calls the image of God in the human soul. The personal God, Krishna, however, now begins to obtrude himself into the Brahman-

Ātman synthesis. Again, as in chapter ii, he is the object on which the Yogin concentrates in order to still his mind; but this time there is a difference, for the Yogin who controls or integrates himself "attains to the peace that culminates in *nirvāna* and which has its basis in me" (6.15). God, then, is the basis of the state of *nirvāna* and therefore of Brahman (which is synonymous with it) not *vice versâ*. The integrated Yogin is compared, as he is by the Buddhists, to an unflickering lamp in a windless place. Seeing the "self" within himself he is filled with joy and thinks there can be no joy greater than this since he has now reached the apex of his soul. "His self integrated by Yoga he sees that self as abiding in all things and all things in that self; he sees the selfsame everywhere" (6.29). This he had conceived of as being the highest bliss, but Krishna now claims this pantheistic vision as his own: "Whoso sees me in all things and all things in me, for him I am not lost, nor is he lost to me" (6.30). What is the significance of this? Both the "transcendent self" and God, being beyond space and time, may be said to pervade all things, but this does not mean complete identity, for were this really so, relationships of any sort would be impossible; and, for Arjuna, this could not conceivably constitute the highest bliss; for, throughout the Great Epic of which the *Gītā* forms an integral part, Arjuna's relationship to Krishna is so close that they are time and again referred to as the "two Krishnas". So Krishna goes on to say: "That Yogin who, holding fast to unity, partakes of me (*bhajati*, from the same root as *bhakti*, "to partake of", hence "to be loyal to, to worship, to be devoted to, to love") as indwelling all beings, wherever he may be, abides in me." Krishna hereby shows that to experience Brahman or *nirvāna* as the timeless principle in the soul is the prelude, subject to God's grace, to sharing in the Being of God himself who is the source from which both Brahman and *nirvāna* proceed; and the soul now realizes that the infinite dimension it has experienced in itself it has not of itself but because it is indwelt by God. Realizing this it can now worship this God in spirit and in truth—this God who is both the source of its own timeless being and the creator of heaven and earth.

## BHAKTI

This is the first we have heard of *bhakti*—that is, the felt participation of the soul in the total being of God rather than the achievement of an individual *nirvāna*. *Bhakti* normally means simply a "loving devotion" to God, and, according to the nondualist Vedāntins, it must cease once liberation is achieved, for, according to them, liberation means the complete identity of the soul with the Absolute which, alone being real, is that of which the personal God is but an illusory appearance. In the *Gītā*, however, *bhakti* only reaches its full significance *after* liberation: it is a step *beyond* the realization of one's transcendent self as Brahman—as unconditioned by space, time, matter, or anything at all in the phenomenal world. And to make this point yet more clear Krishna adds in the very last verse of this chapter: "Of all Yogins he who worships me with faith, his innermost self fixed on me, is, I think, the most integrated of all." Here for the first time in the sacred literature of the Hindus God makes it plain that liberation from our purely human and material condition is not the end of man's spiritual Odyssey, but merely the beginning: the end is a personal union with the personal God. *Bhakti* is both a preparation for liberation and its completion. It is true that the mere contemplation of God in his transcendence is one of the ways by which liberation may be achieved and once it is achieved this may be the end. Indeed it must be the end if the contemplation of God does not arouse any love of him; but if it does, then the mystic will *know* God and recognize him as the all-highest from which even the eternal Brahman proceeds. So in chapter xiv, 26–7, Krishna says: "Whoso reveres me with the unswerving Yoga of *bhakti*, transcending all qualities, is conformed to becoming Brahman, for I am the ground of Brahman, the immortal and imperishable."

It is, however, only in the last chapter that Krishna makes it absolutely clear that it is only *after* the soul has realized itself as Brahman that it is in a fit state to receive the "highest" *bhakti*, that is, a passionate love for God that leaves room for nothing else. Here again total detachment from all transient things, the integration of the personality around the transcendent self, and the complete abandonment of all passions are insisted on as being the indispensable preliminaries to "becoming Brahman". It is, however, only then that the mystic, "having become Brahman, his self serene, . . . the same to all beings, receives the highest *bhakti* to me. By *bhakti* he comes to know me as I am, how great I am, and who. Then, knowing me as I am, he enters me forthwith" (18. 54–5). Contemplation of God as he is in his eternal essence and as the eternal exemplar of the liberated soul, now no longer ceases once liberation has been won, for it is now raised to a higher power by the grace of God (18. 58) who is not content that his elect should merely contemplate their own eternal essences in timeless and solitary bliss but will rather that they should live in fellowship with him—in a fellowship as close as was that of the incarnate God, Krishna, with his friend Arjuna, but now in a new dimension which is no longer human but divine. And so Krishna's final and "most secret" message has no longer anything to do with "becoming Brahman"—a stage which has now been left behind; rather it is the message that Christ was later to proclaim in its fullness but which came to the Hindus with all the force of an amazing revelation—so strange did it seem to them in the light of what had been revealed to them before—the message that God loves man, "Hear my final word," says the incarnate God, "greatly do I desire thee, therefore will I tell thee thy salvation. Bear me [ever] in mind, love me, worship me, and reverence me. Thus shalt thou come to me. I promise thee truly; for thou art dear to me" (18. 64–5).

No longer is a holy indifference the supreme virtue nor is liberation in isolation, "becoming Brahman", the supreme goal but union and communion with God in the bond of love. This, as the text explicitly states (18. 64), is Krishna's "supreme and most secret doctrine of all." So, for the first time, was the message of the love of God proclaimed to the Hindus.

The *Bhagavad-Gītā* is a watershed in the history of Hinduism, for from now on *bhakti* in its various forms becomes the *living* religion of the Indian people. It manifests itself as loving devotion to, adoration of, and communion and union with God manifesting himself either as Vishnu or as Shiva. For the educated Hindu these two gods are ultimately the same; they are twin aspects of the same ineffable reality, seen, as it were, from a different angle.

## VISHNU AND HIS INCARNATIONS

Of the two great gods or, as the Hindus would say, of the two great manifestations of the one true God, it is Vishnu who from time to time becomes incarnate on earth "for the protection of the good and the destruction of evil-doers, and for the [re-] establishment of the law (*dharma*)" (*Bhagavad-Gītā*, 4. 8). His incarnations, some in animal form and some in human, usually number ten, but only two are important. These are his incarnations as Rāma and as Krishna. Of these Rāma is perhaps the less interesting: he is the ideal of Indian chivalry—loyal, patient in adversity, obedient to higher authority, the chastiser of evil powers, the ideal husband, son, and brother. The devotion accorded to him tends to be more restrained and sober than that accorded to Krishna, and this is in accordance with his character.

Krishna is more complex, for the Krishna we meet with in the Great Epic (of which the *Bhagavad-Gītā* forms part) is different from the Krishna of popular devotion. Even in the Epic he is wayward and in the great war between the Pāndavas and Kauravas he is not above resorting to stratagems which shock his friends and of which he is subsequently ashamed. When the war is over and the Pāndavas are victorious—though the slaughter has been so terrific that little is left them over which to reign—Krishna returns to his tribe; and his death is tragic. For no sooner has he returned home than the tribesmen, besotted with wine, go berserk and slaughter one another right down to the last man. Krishna, saddened and apparently a failure, retires to the seashore to meditate. A passing fowler, mistaking him for a gazelle, shoots him in the heel, although, as the Epic points out, being God, he could have easily saved himself. The apparent failure of the incarnate God and his subsequent ascension into

heaven to resume his reign cannot but put us in mind of the
Passion, Resurrection and Ascension of Our Lord.

The Krishna of popular religion is, however, very different
from the Krishna of the Great Epic. He appears as a handsome
and wayward boy, brought up among cowherds, and his amours
with the cowherds' daughters who are distraught with the love
of him, are the subject of endless stories. These stories, we are
told, are allegories of God's love for human souls and their love
for him; and this love is passionate, the soul being unable to bear
separation from him for a single moment. In the Krishna cult
the "passionless" ideal of Buddhism and the earlier Hinduism
has been completely abandoned. Where there is love there must
also be attachment and passion, and even the philosopher,
Rāmānuja, the first and greatest intellectual apologist for the
*bhakti* cults, declares that God too cannot bear separation from
the soul. "Whoever loves me beyond measure," God is represented as saying, "him will I love beyond measure [in return].
Unable to bear separation from him, I cause him to possess me."
God needs the soul as much as the soul needs God, and this
means that the soul is neither annihilated nor absorbed in the
liberated state, but experiences unending and ever-increasing
love. "[The devotee,]" Krishna is made to say, "though he has
come to possess me, is not himself destroyed, and though I give
myself to one who worships me in this wise, it seems to me that I
have done nothing for him." Krishna's love is unconditional.

It was above all in South India that this new religion of the
love of God spread. There the worshippers of Krishna called
themselves *Ālvārs* or "men who have intuitive knowledge of
God". These men broke with traditional religion in two ways;
first they flouted the caste system which constituted the social
framework through which the Hindu religion operated, and
secondly they denied that liberation from time and matter constituted man's highest goal. With great subtlety they distinguished a mysticism of the soul as such from the mysticism of the
love of God. "It is not possible", wrote Nāmm'ālvār, the greatest
of them all, "to give a description of that wonderful entity, the
soul—the soul which is eternal, and is essentially characterized

by intelligence—the soul which the Lord has condescended to exhibit to me as a mode of himself—or I am related to him as is the predicate to the subject, or attribute to substance." The soul, then, is in some sense an aspect of God—a minute fraction of him as the *Bhagavad-Gītā* puts it—it is eternal and necessarily indestructible because it is independent of the passage of time. This, however, does not mean that it is autarchic and totally independent as the Sāṁkhya-Yoga and the non-dualist Vedānta taught. On the contrary, it is totally dependent on God: God is its origin and its goal, and it must therefore aspire to God with its whole being. *Moksha* or "liberation" is not man's final goal: it is only his final goal *quâ* man, not his final goal as a potentially divine being. In Christian terminology liberation marks the end of the *via purgativa*, it is the cleansing of the mirror of the soul of all the dust and dirt of sin: it is a state of peace, timeless and "empty", detached from all earthly things and indifferent. It is, however, not quite the *total* detachment of the Sāṁkhya-Yoga, for a longing for God remains. And so "through cessation of all inclination to other things and the increase of longing for God *in a timeless and spaceless manner*, and through the pangs of separation in not realizing him constantly, he considers himself as a woman, and through the pangs of love loses consciousness". In this way the soul passes beyond and out of the consciousness of its own existential unity and timelessness and enters into a relationship of passionate love with Krishna, the heavenly bridegroom. In this relationship it must play a woman's part—and some of the medieval Christian mystics have used just this image —it must remain wholly passive as it awaits the embrace of the divine lover. The soul of itself does nothing, it is God who acts in and through it. With the Ālvārs the sexual imagery gives no more offence than the same imagery so constantly used by the Christian mystics. Indeed it is only because the whole mystery of sexuality has been so shamefully degraded in the West that the elevation of sex on to a religious plane appears so shocking to some puritan minds. Of course excesses have occurred from time to time, but the Hindu attitude towards sexual union as being something essentially holy is much more sane than that of the

puritans; for, if man is made in the image of God, then the sexual
act must in some way reflect something that is divine. For both
the Hindu and the Christian mystics it reflects the "spiritual
espousals" of God with the soul.

## SHIVA, THE GREAT LORD

This new mysticism of the love of God was not confined to the
worshippers of Vishnu, the God who from time to time becomes
incarnate "for the protection of the good and the destruction of
evil-doers and for the [re-]establishment of the law". The worshippers of the far more terrible God, Shiva, were not slow to
follow suit.

Shiva is the God in whom all the opposites meet and are
resolved into unity. He is ithyphallic yet perpetually chaste: he is
creator and destroyer, terrible and mild, the source of evil as well
as good, both male and female, both eternal rest and ceaseless
activity. In his terrible manifestation he is "Lord of the Dance";
he dances creation into existence and he dances the destruction
of the world. In the dance of destruction he careers down the
mountain-side like a drunkard or a madman, surrounded by
half-human, half-animal creatures who urge him on in his career
of destruction. Or again he is said to be most at home in the
cremation-ground, his neck encircled with a necklace of skulls,
his matted locks alive with snakes. It seems strange to us that
such a God could have inspired a devotion as fervid at least as
that accorded to Vishnu in his incarnations as Rāma and
Krishna, and yet he did; and it is in the hymns addressed to
Shiva by his worshippers in South India that we find a spirituality more nearly Christian, perhaps, than anything we find
elsewhere in non-Christian lands.

In theology the worshippers of Shiva break with the extreme
monism of the non-dualist Vedānta even more violently than do
the worshippers of Vishnu. It may be remembered that the word
used by the Sāmkhya-Yoga to represent liberation was "isolation"—the isolation of the soul in its essence apart from all
created things and from God. This for the Shiva-worshippers of

South India is the *lowest* state of the soul in its progress towards union with God. All the words hitherto used to describe the liberated soul here re-appear: "the soul is non-intelligent, it is formless, imperishable, . . . it is actionless, markless, it is not a self-agent; it cannot enjoy fruits; . . . it is omnipresent" (*Śiva-jñāna-siddhiyār* 3. 4. 38). All the attributes, in fact, that had been used to describe the highest Brahman-Ātman are here used to describe the soul in its most undeveloped state; and this is surely no accident. The state of a pure negative "isolation" and un-differentiated oneness which was the goal of the Sāṁkhya-Yoga and the non-dualist Vedānta is really no more than the state of a human embryo before consciousness arises. So far from being the highest state, it is the lowest, being inferior to the next stage in which the soul is united to a body. This bodily state is, as in Christianity, a time of testing in which the soul must rid itself of all egoism and all that attaches it to matter. In this God graci-ously assists the soul and, like a loving father, leads it to its heavenly home.

> Just as the king's son [we read] taken and brought up among savages did not know himself to be different from the others till his true father came and, separating him from his wild associates, acknowledged him as his own and had him respected even as him-self; so also does our Lord appearing as the gracious spiritual director separate the sorrowing soul which is caught among the savages of the five senses and is unable to know its own greatness or that of this Friend from its sensory environments; he purifies it of its dross and, transforming it even into his own glory, places it under his flowery feet (*ibid.*, 3.8.1).

God, then, is the father of the soul and in this sense there is identity of substance between them, but this does not mean that there can be complete identity between God and the soul since a feeling of creatureliness will always remain. The mystical union is spoken of either as "conjunction" or as "conformity" or as "proximity". "They will so unite with God that they will never leave God, and God will never leave them; and dwelling in him, they will perceive only God in everything" (*ibid.*, 3. 8. 29). We find the same idea in Simone Weil and many other Western mystics. Of precisely such a mystical state she writes: "Such a love does not love beings and things in God; it loves them from God's standpoint (*de chez Dieu*). Being in God's presence it looks down from there on all beings and all things, its very looking being commingled with God's looking" (*Attente de Dieu*, p. 65). The soul, entering into the fullness of God, "becomes one with that fullness and all in all"; it melts in God as iron melts in fire and is transformed into it. It is not destroyed but transformed into a higher mode of being. United with God all its actions will henceforth be divine. For "in order that men may know him the Lord gives his devotees his form, and they know him and are in him. So he is visible in his devotees who know him, as ghee is visible in curds" (*Śiva-jñāna-bodham*, 12. 3). Union with God therefore means so complete a transformation of the personality that it is now God who acts through the saint, the saint being completely passive in his hands. The same idea we also find in the medieval Christian mystics. Henry Suso, for instance, a German mystic of the fourteenth century, writes: "In so far as man remains in himself, he can fall into sin, as St John says: 'If we say that we have no sin, we deceive ourselves, and the truth is not in us.' But in so far as he does not remain in himself, he does not commit sin, as St John says in his Epistle, that the man who is born of God does not sin, nor err, for the divine seed remains in him" (*The Little Book of Truth*, p. 196).

In other words the man who has cleansed the image of God which is his true self of all the egoism and selfishness it derives from his purely human self and who is indwelt by God, cannot, so long as this condition lasts, fall into sin, for sin, among other things, means separation; and there is no separation here.

It has often been said that in Hinduism there is little sense of sin; and up to a point this is true. But here again it was not true among the worshippers of Shiva in South India where we meet with a sense of the human being's utter unworthiness in the face of the divine righteousness and majesty that is reminiscent of the great Reformers. Take these stanzas written in the ninth century for instance:

The meanest cur am I; I know not how to do the right;
'Twere but what I deserve, should'st Thou my wickedness requite
With the dread fate of those who never saw Thy flowery feet;
For though mine eyes have seen, my ears have heard saints guileless
  meet,
Who reached Thy fragrant presence, yet I stay, for false am I,
Fit for naught save to eat and dress, Lion of victory. . . .
Since I am false, and false my heart, and false my very love,
Howe'er I weep, still held by deeds, can I reach Thee above?
O honey, nectar, O essential sweetness, great as sweet,
Grant grace to me to find the path that leads unto Thy feet.

>               (F. Kingsbury and G. E. Phillips, *Hymns of the*
>                         *Tamil Saivite Saints*, pp. 95–7.)

More striking still in its sense of utter unworthiness is the
following:

Evil, all evil my race, evil my qualities all,
Great am I only in sin, evil is even my good.
Evil my innermost self, foolish, avoiding the pure,
Beast am I not, yet the ways of the beast I can never forsake.
I can exhort with strong words, telling men what they should hate,
Yet I can never give gifts, only to beg them I know.
Ah! wretched man that I am, whereunto came I to birth?

>                                         (*Ibid.*, p. 47.)

This is a new note in Indian religion. In the *Bhagavad-Gītā*
indeed we are shown for the first time man's utter nothingness in
the face of the majesty of God, and when Arjuna beholds Krishna
in glory, he is terrified at the awful vision, but his is a sense not so
much of unworthiness as of impotence. With these worshippers
of Shiva in the early Middle Ages, on the other hand, it is a sense
of unworthiness that prevails and of wonder that so holy a God
should stoop to consider something so vile, that he should love
it, and that he should summon it to share in his very being:

Thou gav'st Thyself, Thou gained'st me;
  Which did the better bargain drive?
Bliss found I in infinity;
  But what didst Thou from me derive?

O Shiva, Perundurai's God,
My mind Thou tookest for Thy shrine:
My very body's Thine abode:
What can I give Thee, Lord, of mine?

*(Ibid.*, p. 117.)

## ORTHODOXY AND CASTE

The *bhakti* movement starts with the *Bhagavad-Gītā* in perhaps the third century B.C. and it continues to grow and spread
abroad—developing here and there some wild extravagances—
right down to the eighteenth century. It develops alongside of
and in rivalry with orthodox Brāhmanism which is the official
sacrificial and sacramental system controlled and administered
by the priestly caste, the Brāhmans.

The caste system in India finds few defenders among enlightened Hindus today; but at a very early date it had become
ossified, and orthodoxy lent religious sanction to this rigidly
stratified social system which perpetuated and sanctified social
privilege and social degradation that would scarcely have been
tolerated in any other society. Neither Buddhism which rose and
fell in India between the sixth century B.C. and the sixth century
A.D. nor the *bhakti* sects had been able to break it down,
although the Buddhist ethic, which so greatly stressed the gentler
virtues of non-violence and compassion, had been absorbed into
the Hindu bloodstream and had, in theory at least, done much
to alleviate the wrongs suffered by the lower castes and outcastes.
The justification of the system, which relegates whole sectors of
the population to permanent degradation, is that birth into a
given caste depends on the deeds one has performed in past lives.
If, then, a man is born an outcaste, this can only mean that he
has committed fearful crimes in former lives; his degraded state
in this life is therefore no more than the just price a man pays
for former sins. So deep was this belief in transmigration that,
as often as not, the outcaste himself would accept his lot as being
in the natural order of things, and it was only with the coming
of the Muslims in successive waves from the eleventh to the
fourteenth century that the outcastes were able to improve their

position by embracing Islam. The marvel is not that so many did but rather that so many preferred to remain within the Hindu fold.

## ENCOUNTER WITH THE WEST

When the British in their turn arrived in India, they found Hinduism at a very low ebb, and the early missionaries thought that the conversion of India might well be imminent. The impact of the missionaries and particularly of the Protestants was very great, for no two religions could be more different. Whether it had intended to do so or not, Protestantism had eviscerated Christianity of that mystical kernel which still lives on in the Catholic Mass, and the type of Christianity that made its impact on nineteenth-century India was decidedly this-worldly—laying great stress on good works and social organization for the relief of the needy and the education of the ignorant. It is no exaggeration to say that Protestantism gave India a social conscience it had not possessed before. This, however, did not result in any wholesale conversions; it merely resulted in Hinduism reforming itself on Christian ethical lines. The Christian missionaries made the great mistake of assuming that they were in all respects superior to the Hindus and they were thus, with few exceptions, not prepared to take these "idol-worshippers" seriously. The Hindus, on their side, who have always tended to identify true religion with mysticism, found Protestantism stilted and barren: they could not see that their mentors were making any contact with the Eternal in any form (and this, surely, is the whole point of religion). They seemed rooted in time and altogether too busy with their good works and charities in a wretched and transient world from which it was the business of *their* religion to escape. The Jesus of the synoptic Gospels they were prepared to accept just as they had been prepared to accept the Buddha—on their own terms. He might be *a* son of God or *an* incarnation of God, but they could not accept him as the sole incarnation of God. After all there was nothing particularly extraordinary about incarnation and they could see little difference between him and Krishna. Moreover, the Hindu mind, though receptive of almost any new idea, has singularly little patience with dogma. After all, the Muslims had invaded their country, bringing with them their religion which they also claimed was the one true religion, and here were these Christians, whom in any case the Muslims despised, coming and making the self-same claim on behalf of *their* religion. For their part they could not see what all the fuss was about, and, following the Vedānta tradition, they were quite prepared to respect these religions as being different paths leading to the same goal, but they declined to believe that any of them was the only path.

The missionaries, on their side, were not slow to point out the gross abuses that had become embedded in Hinduism—the burning of widows, child marriages, temple prostitution, and the scandal of untouchability. Enlightened opinion in India was stung into action by missionary propaganda and agitated for the legal abolition of these abuses. Gradually—except in the case of untouchability—the Government acquiesced in their demands, but it was only after India had won her independence that the scandal of untouchability became illegal.

This is no place to enumerate the various reform movements that sprang up within Hinduism in the course of the nineteenth century. We need only note that the *bhakti* cults which, at their highest, came so near to Catholic Christianity in its mystical aspect, had themselves degenerated into a purely emotional religion, and the bridge that might have been built between the Indian soul and the Catholic Church was thus no longer standing. Moreover, the frequently arrogant attitude of the nineteenth-century missionaries was bound sooner or later to produce a swing of the pendulum away from and against Christianity in all its manifestations.

## NEO-VEDĀNTA: RĀMAKRISHNA AND VIVEKĀNANDA

Earlier in this chapter we had occasion to mention the non-dualist Vedānta. This school of philosophy of which the great ninth-century philosopher, Shankara, was the greatest exponent, maintained that the experience of unfractionable oneness that

Yogic meditation could induce meant that the innermost essence of man, his ātman or transcendent self was identical with Brahman, the Absolute and ground of the universe: apart from this Brahman-Ātman nothing really existed at all. As to God, in so far as he was creator of the world and thereby involved in the temporal process, he, being distinct from the One Brahman-Ātman (which is beyond time), must, from the point of view of absolute Reality, himself be an illusion or at best an "appearance".

The earlier reform movements, though they rejected Christian theology, had nonetheless accepted a monotheistic rather than a pantheistic or monistic view of the universe: they had sought to reform Hinduism along Protestant Christian lines. In the middle of the nineteenth century, however, there appeared a figure who was to inject new self-confidence into Hinduism and whose disciples were, for the first time in history, to propagate its more esoteric teachings abroad. This was Rāmakrishna Paramahaṁsa.

During the great period of Indian philosophy the representatives of the leading schools would argue with each other with considerable heat. Rāmakrishna, however, changed the whole climate of Hinduism. Irritated, as were most Hindus, by the exclusive claims of Christianity, he retaliated not by condemning Christianity, but by saying that all religions were true—each in its own way. Rāmakrishna was, moreover, a visionary, and his visions would vary with the company he kept. Among Hindus he experienced, or claimed to have experienced, the presence of Krishna or Rāma; when among Muslims he is said to have had a vision of Muhammad, while a study of the New Testament duly induced a vision of Christ. All these visions, he thought, stemmed from the same source; the differences were superficial. Christianity, like all other religions, was one way among many and, in its proper place, a very good one, but it was questionable whether its proper place was the holy land of India.

Rāmakrishna had a particularly strong devotion to the goddess Kālī, Shiva's terrible consort, who was and is much worshipped in his native Bengal. He had had many visions of her, and his attachment to her amounted almost to an obsession. He had, however, been schooled in the non-dualist Vedānta, and he was therefore persuaded that his visions and the goddess herself whom he called the Divine Mother were something very much less than the supreme Truth. If this was to be reached at all, then the Divine Mother herself would have to be eliminated along with all that was other than the One. To experience the One who alone is, even the most sublime appearances must be eliminated. And so Rāmakrishna is reported as saying: "With a stern determination I again sat to meditate, and as soon as the gracious form of the Divine Mother appeared before me, I used my discrimination as a sword and with it severed it into two. There remained no more obstruction to my mind, which at once soared beyond the relative plane, and I lost myself in samādhi (trance)."

The implications of this are obvious. The One alone exists absolutely; all else is appearance. God, the highest appearance of the One, is himself not absolutely real, and he therefore appears in a different form to different peoples at different stages of development. In India he has appeared as Rāma and Krishna, as Shiva and his consort Kālī. To the Jews he appeared as Yahweh, to the Muslims as Allah, whereas to the Christians he appeared as the Incarnate Christ. None of these appearances has any more validity than the others, and conversion from one religion to another is therefore both futile and wrong. True religion is simply the experience of the timeless and transcendent; dogmas and rituals—except in so far as they induce a direct contact with the unseen—are irrelevant. There seemed little evidence that the Protestant missionaries, for all their preaching, had had any direct experience of the God they preached, let alone of "liberation", the nature of which they did not even understand. Their preaching of a higher morality (if such it was) was no doubt all very well in its way, but even philanthropy is of little use unless it leads to liberation. "By these philanthropic activities," he is recorded as saying, "you are really doing good to yourself. If you can do them disinterestedly, your mind will become pure and you will develop love of God. As soon as you have that love, you will realize him."

There is much in the Upanishads and the Great Epic about transcending good and evil; and this danger, which can lead to the denial of any moral code as being purely relative, is liable to appear in any form of mysticism: hence the Buddha's insistence on the absolute necessity of practising the virtues of non-violence, compassion and friendliness if *nirvāna* is to be achieved at all. For Rāmakrishna, however, good and evil cease to have any meaning once liberation has been achieved. Evil itself is only an appearance, and God indwells the swindler and the lecher as much as he does the honest man.

Rāmakrishna had what is nowadays called a charismatic presence. He not only had visionary and mystical experiences in profusion; he was also capable of transmitting them to others. Of these Swami Vivekānanda was by far the most notable, for it was he who spread his master's ideas in America and Europe and who founded the Rāmakrishna mission with its many centres in the States and elsewhere and its monastic houses in India itself.

In 1893 Vivekānanda attended the first session of the World Parliament of Religions at Chicago where he created a sensation. Hitherto Hinduism had had to defend itself against unremitting attack first from the Muslims and secondly from the Christians. Now for the first time, in the person of Vivekānanda, it moved on to the offensive. Even more than his master he saw nothing but evil and arrogance in the Christian attempts to win converts. "Do I wish that the Christian would become a Hindu?" he exclaimed, "God forbid. . . . The Christian is not to become a Hindu or a Buddhist, nor a Hindu or a Buddhist to become a Christian. But each religion must assimilate the spirit of the others and yet preserve its individuality and grow according to its own law of growth." There is much wisdom in this saying, and in our last chapter we shall try to analyse just what a Catholic can assimilate and what he cannot.

Throughout this chapter we have tried to show how, in the main stream of religious thought and practice, the worship of God, either as Shiva or as Vishnu in one of his incarnations, came to replace the older ideal of finding the immortal spark within oneself. We have also pointed out the radical difference between the non-dualist Vedāntins who regard the achievement of "liberation" as the ultimate goal of man and the theists who regard it only as a preliminary to a personal contact with the personal God which continues even after liberation has been won. Vivekānanda succeeded in swinging Hinduism back from the theistic outlook of the *bhakti* sects to the strict non-dualism of Shankara. If man is indeed identical with the Absolute, then he bears his destiny in his own hands: he transcends all the opposites; he is beyond good and evil; he is omnipotent. Man is the Absolute, God only an appearance. And so he says:

> When we have nobody to grope towards, no devil to lay our blame upon, no Personal God to carry our burdens, when we are alone responsible, then we shall rise to our highest and best. I am responsible for my fate, I am the bringer of good unto myself, I am the bringer of evil. I am the Pure and Blessed One. . . . I have neither death nor fear, I have neither caste nor creed. I have neither father nor mother nor brother, neither friend nor foe, for I am Existence, Knowledge, and Bliss Absolute; I am the Blissful One, I am the Blissful One. I am not bound either by virtue or vice, by happiness or misery. Pilgrimages and books and ceremonials can never bind me. I have neither hunger nor thirst; the body is not mine, nor am I subject to the superstitions and decay that come from the body. I am Existence, Knowledge, and Bliss Absolute; I am the Blissful One, I am the Blissful One (*Jnana-Yoga*, pp. 231–2).

One can imagine the attraction that such a creed could exercise on many who, like Aldous Huxley, had rejected the Christian God with loathing and who were yet looking for a religion without dogma which could satisfy their ineradicable craving for an eternal verity. In this revived form of the Vedānta and in Zen Buddhism they were to find it.

Despite Vivekānanda, however, the general trend of Hinduism towards not only theism, but an ever more responsible and moralistic theism, was to continue and was to receive a new impetus from one of the greatest men of our century, Mahatma Gandhi, who did more than anyone else to win his country's freedom—and that without resort to violence.

## *MAHATMA GANDHI AND NON-VIOLENCE*

Right up to the nineteenth century Hinduism can be said to have been a lopsided religion in that it attached overwhelming importance to the mystical side of religion, little to the practical and moral. It was so other-worldly that it allowed a social system to grow up which created artificial barriers between man and man and degraded millions of human beings—the outcastes or untouchables—to a status that was little, if at all, better than that of the animals. Indian man had become so intent on escaping into a timeless state that transcended good and evil that he had little time to consider the right ordering of *this* world.

For Gandhi things were very different. Though certainly a man of prayer he did not attach the overwhelming importance to liberation as such that Rāmakrishna had done. He was interested in improving the lot of his fellow-men here and now; and so he could say: "To me God is Truth and Love; God is ethics and morality; God is fearlessness; God is the source of Light and Life, and yet he is above and beyond all these. *God is conscience.*"

This view of God he had learnt from the missionaries, from reading the Sermon on the Mount, and from Tolstoy. God as ethics and morality and as conscience had not hitherto been a Hindu idea. But Gandhi, though he always considered himself an orthodox Hindu, did not regard himself as being bound by the letter of the law. If God was conscience, then the conscience of a man of truth must take precedence over anything the Hindu scriptures might say.

My belief in the Hindu scriptures [he wrote] does not require me to accept every word and every verse as divinely inspired. Nor do I claim to have any first-hand knowledge of these wonderful books. But I do claim to know and feel the truths of the essential teaching of the Scriptures. I decline to be bound by any interpretation, however learned it may be, if it is repugnant to reason and moral sense.

Yet Gandhi was never tempted to become a Christian. He was happy to follow the ethics of selflessness and non-violence he found in the Sermon on the Mount, for he was already familiar with the similar ethics of the Buddhists and Jains so much of which had already been absorbed into Hinduism; but he was repelled by the exclusive claims of Christianity, by its insistence that Christ was the only incarnation of God, and by the whole theological frame in which Christianity was set. It is unfortunate that his early Christian contacts were often with extreme and sometimes aberrant Protestant sects; for not only did their services bore him, he could not find in them even an atmosphere that he felt to be religious. There was plenty of preaching and plenty of moral exhortation but no inward communion with the divine. To the best of my knowledge the only time he felt this specifically numinous atmosphere and this sense of the holy in a Christian church was in Notre Dame in Paris which he visited in 1890 when he was still a law student in London. The Catholics were after all just as much "idol-worshippers" as the Hindus; but, as Gandhi remarked, "the devout souls kneeling before the Virgin could not be worshipping mere marble. They were fired with genuine devotion and they worshipped not stone, but the divinity of which it was symbolic. I have an impression that I felt then that by this worship they were not detracting from, but increasing, the glory of God."

It is unfortunate that Gandhi had so little contact with Catholic missionaries, for he would surely have seen that the mystery at the heart of Catholicism is not unlike the mystery at the heart of Hinduism—the mystery of the unity of all things in their Creator. As it was, his principal contacts were all with Protestants, and his criticism both of them as human beings and of the crude methods they employed makes disturbing reading. Addressing them in Calcutta he had said: "I miss receptiveness, humility, willingness on your part to identify yourselves with the masses of India;" and this must have been a bitter pill to swallow for men who claimed to follow in the footsteps of One who had humbled himself even to the shameful death of the Cross.

One of the things with which the Reformers reproached the Church was that she withheld the Word of God from the laity. Yet it is more than arguable that indiscriminate and untutored reading of the Bible can be very dangerous indeed, so greatly do some of the older Old Testament stories conflict with New

Testament morality; and we all know that the South Africans justify their treatment of the Negroes by the supposed analogy of the conquering Israelites' treatment of the conquered and displaced peoples of the promised land.

Protestants once thought that you had only to put the "Good Book" into the hands of a non-Christian for him to be converted. Were he not, then there must be something seriously wrong with him and he would therefore be consigned to eternal perdition. A naïve Christian from Manchester tried to do precisely this with Gandhi. "Do please read the Bible," he said, without giving any indication as to which portions would be most profitable for him in the beginning. Gandhi, not unnaturally, supposed he was to start at the beginning and read through to the end. His account of the experience is not without interest:

> I began reading it [he writes] but I could not possibly read through the Old Testament. I read the book of Genesis, and the chapters that followed invariably sent me to sleep. But just for the sake of being able to say that I had read it, I plodded through the other books with much difficulty and without the least interest or understanding. I disliked reading the book of Numbers.

The New Testament pleased him better and the Sermon on the Mount went straight to his heart. All that appealed to his conscience he could accept, and so he "tried to unify the teaching of the *Gītā*, *The Light of Asia* and the Sermon on the Mount". In all of these he saw that renunciation is the highest form of religion; and by renunciation and the selfless service of his people he was in the end to win his country's independence from an arrogant and money-loving power that still presumed to call itself Christian.

Christianity has so far failed in India because Christians so rarely practise what they preach: there has been too little renunciation, and it is renunciation above all things that goes straight to the Indian heart. Gandhi succeeded because he did just this, and his criticism of Christians on ethical grounds as well is not unjust. In what way were these men who claimed to represent a God of Love different from other men?

The pious lives of Christians [he wrote] did not give me anything that the lives of men of other faiths had failed to give. I had seen in other lives just the same reformation that I had heard of among Christians. Philosophically there was nothing extraordinary in Christian principles. From the point of view of sacrifice, it seemed to me that the Hindus greatly surpassed the Christians.

Christianity, as preached and practised by the missionaries in India, had nothing to offer Gandhi. Only the Sermon on the Mount could he take to his heart. In doing this he added something new to Hinduism. He did not become a Christian, but he brought something of Christ to the Hindus: he brought a conscience that had been largely conditioned by Christian influences into a civilization that had for long centuries been unmoved by what he called the "curse" of untouchability.

Thanks to Gandhi's unremitting propaganda and example the Hindu temples were finally thrown open to the untouchables, and with the establishment of the independent Republic of India, untouchability at last became illegal. Gandhi had infused a Christian conscience into the ancient creed, but he did not wish to do away with the sacramental framework of that creed since he saw, rightly, that this was what held it together. He saw Hinduism as the *national* religion of India just as Judaism is the national religion of the Jews. It was, then, he thought, the duty of the enlightened Hindu to preserve in it all that might be preserved, but to root out whatever offended his social conscience. Thus he offered lip-service to the caste system in its original and inoffensive form, the veneration of images, the domestic rites that orthodox Hindus were expected to perform in their homes, and the veneration of the cow. He saw that the Hindu rites in home and temple, performed in the presence of images representing some aspect of the divine, were the very cement that held Hinduism together. Do away with these, and you do away with Hinduism. Gandhi accepted religions as they are: they are the organizations of finite human beings the purpose of which is, through rites and ceremonies and symbols, to lift finite man out of his purely temporal dimension into a state of being that transcends time. Each and all of them are true—and imperfect; and because they are imperfect, they must aim at perfecting themselves rather than at converting individuals from another faith. A religion can only demonstrate its truth or superiority by the holiness of the individuals that go to make it up; and in Gandhi's opinion the Christians in India made a very poor showing. He, however, shamed us Christians by leading a life of self-denial and self-forgetfulness that few of us would even dare to attempt.

Gandhi remained a Hindu to the end of his days—but he had introduced into Hinduism a moral earnestness that had not been there before. He did not seek to reach a state that was beyond time and therefore beyond good and evil as others had done before him. He knew that evil must be faced and combated and that this can only be done by turning the other cheek, by self-control, and by strict adherence to the truth as he understood it. The mystery of iniquity he did not try to solve: he tried to overcome it with goodness.

> I call God long-suffering and patient [he wrote] precisely because he permits evil in the world. I know that he has no evil. He is the author of it and yet untouched by it.
>
> I know too that I shall never know God if I do not wrestle with and against evil even at the cost of life itself. I am fortified in this belief by my own humble and limited experience. The purer I try to become, the nearer I feel to be to God. How much more should I be, when my faith is not a mere apology as it is today but has become as immovable as the Himalayas and as white and bright as the snows on their peaks.

Gandhi was a man of God, and he was also a man who saw good in all religions. He was not ashamed to learn from Christianity and Islam, nor was he blind to the sometimes hideous defects of his own religion. He learnt much from Christianity, and with his example before us we should be presumptuous fools to think that we, as Catholics, have nothing to learn from him and from the whole religious tradition that made him possible.

# CHAPTER II

# CHINA AND JAPAN

In our introductory chapter we pointed out the curious fact that there are two nations, and two only, from which the great religions of the world overwhelmingly derive. The Jews have always claimed that they are the chosen people, and in recent times this exclusivity has been resented, particularly in India; for the Indian contribution to the religious life of the world has been as great and as durable as that of Israel. If indeed Israel is a chosen race, then, many Indians thought, had they not too some claim to election? This claim was in fact made by one of the nineteenth-century reformers, Mahadev Govind Ranade, who declared: "I profess implicit faith in two articles of my creed. This country of ours is the true land of promise. This race of ours is the chosen race. . . . If the miraculous preservation of a few thousand Jews had a purpose, this more miraculous preservation of one fifth of the human race is not due to mere chance."

The Indians are and always have been an intensely religious people, and their religious Odyssey is one of perpetual quest for the living God: but throughout its history there have been two tensions in Hinduism which to this day remain unresolved. We dwelt at some length in the last chapter on the tension between the theists on the one hand and the monists on the other. Was there a personal God so transcendent that he transcended the impersonal Absolute, Brahman, which the mystic experiences in and as his authentic, "transcendent self", or was this God merely an appearance of the Absolute? The whole *bhakti* tradition affirmed with passion that the personal God, Shiva or Vishnu, was prior to the Absolute itself, while the non-dualist Vedāntins, who enjoy a certain vogue in America today, affirmed precisely the opposite. The second tension in Hinduism is that between the official religion which depends for the administration of its "sacraments", that is, the rites performed over the faithful at all the crucial turning-points in his life from conception to crema-tion, by the Brāhman priests, and the inner religion the goal of which is the liberation of the individual soul from temporal life and these very rites that mark its passing. When all is said and done, however, Hindu orthodoxy regards the religious rites as little better than magic, for the accomplished man of the three higher classes or castes will lay aside all rites as no longer serving any useful purpose once he feels the approach of liberation. Man's salvation is not of this world, it is from this world. This is made even more clear in Buddhism than it is in Hinduism. Both are in essence "other-worldly" religions.

## CONFUCIANISM

In China things were very different. The Chinese have never thought of themselves as being a particularly religious people: they are practical, hard-working, and have their feet firmly on the ground. Confucianism, which was the official religion of China for a thousand years before the revolution of 1911 when it was swept away, has indeed rarely been regarded as being a religion at all. It is certainly not a religion in the Western sense, that is, it is little concerned with God or the after-life, nor is it a religion in the Indian sense since it is quite unconcerned with the uncovering of the "transcendent self" that indwells the empirical soul. Rather it is concerned with right-living within a well-ordered and hierarchical society, the apex of which is the Emperor, the "Son of Heaven".

Another characteristic of the two major indigenous Chinese "religions", Confucianism and Taoism, is that they see the earthly paradise not in the future but in the past: they do not so much look forward to a new Jerusalem as look back to the Garden of Eden as it was before Adam fell. The Confucians look back to the legendary "philosopher kings", Yao and Shun, and their successors as the model which all rulers should imitate. It was for this reason that Confucius said of himself: "I have trans-mitted what was taught to me without making up anything of my own" (*Analects*, 7. 1). Confucius, then, claimed to be no more than the interpreter of the ancient books or "Classics" which were said to have been handed down from the times of Yao and Shun on. The ideal state of society which is said to have lasted from Yao till shortly before the time of Confucius is called *tao*, the (ideal) "way" of government.

## THE TAO OF CONFUCIANISM

Both Confucianism and Taoism accept a Tao or "Way" as being the natural law of the universe. This Tao is also referred to as the "Will of Heaven"; and the Will of Heaven represents the proper functioning of all things in the context of the whole —"heaven-and-earth" as they call it. To govern properly it is essential to govern in accordance with the Tao, and, since the Tao is the moral law as applicable to man as well as the natural law observable throughout nature, it is important to know what this moral law is. This, according to the Confucians, is to be found in the six "Classics", in the sayings of Confucius (the *Analects*), and in those of his most famous disciple, Mencius, who lived some two hundred years after him. The moral law is based on right human relationships, and these are "the affection that should exist between father and son, the righteousness that acts as a bond between sovereign and subject, the division of duties between husband and wife, the rules of precedence between old and young, and mutual fidelity between friends" (*Mencius*, tr. L. Giles, p. 61).

## FILIAL PIETY AND GOODNESS

"Honour thy father and mother," we are commanded in the Decalogue. The Confucians go much further, for they make filial piety the supreme virtue from which all others stem, for "he who loves his parents does not dare to hate others. He who reverences his parents does not dare to act contemptuously toward others. By love and reverence being perfectly fulfilled in the service of his parents, his moral influence is shed upon the people and he becomes a pattern for all the border nations. This is the filial piety of the Son of Heaven" (*Hsiao Ching*, 2).

Filial piety is the supreme natural virtue from which all others spring. The proper relationship between father and son shows us what the proper relationship between prince and subject ought to be. "Just as the connecting link between serving one's father and serving one's mother is love, so is the connecting between serving one's father and serving one's prince reverence" (*ibid.*, 5). Whatever the relationship may be it must be inspired by the great Confucian virtue *jên*, "goodness", sometimes translated "human-heartedness" or "benevolence". This, according to the great majority of Confucians, is natural to man: to be truly human, one must also be humane. This, however, does not mean an indiscriminate love of all creatures equally, as the philosopher Mo Ti had taught, for this goes against the natural Tao. Unlike the Buddhists with their excessive respect for animal life the Confucians considered that though it is proper to be kind to animals, to love them equally with humans would be to stray from the Tao. "The higher type of man treats animals with kindness, but not with the same sort of benevolence that he shows to the people; which, again, is different from the personal affection that he shows to his parents. He is loving to his parents and benevolent to the people; benevolent to the people and kind to animals" (*Mencius*, p. 117). These relationships are in the nature of things and to try to change them is to pervert the true Tao. Similarly, in the State, which is simply the family on an enormously extended scale, good government depends on everyone being what he is and fulfilling his functions in the spirit of human-heartedness and righteousness. "Let the prince be a prince, the minister a minister, the father a father and the son a son," Confucius said (*Analects*, 12. 11), and we see what he meant.

*Jên* is the ideal of pure goodness attained in the ideal days of the philosopher kings but never attained since; it is the perfect putting into practice of the Confucian Tao which itself is based on right relationships of give and take within every social unit from the family right up to the Celestial Empire itself. It results in effortless co-operation and harmony in which each works both for his own self-perfection and for the perfection of the whole. Heaven and earth work together and man is the mid-point between them, and in so far as he effortlessly co-operates with them he forms a trinity with them, and in fulfilling his own human Tao, which is based on moral excellence, he co-operates in the universal harmony of all things. To be yourself fully is the role that Heaven has allotted you: that is how you may best follow the Tao. The ruler himself should not always be busying himself about things that it is the duty of his ministers to do: *his* business is to be good and by setting an example to others to radiate his own goodness among them. "If the ruler himself is upright," Confucius said, "all will go well even though he does not give orders. But if he himself is not upright, even though he gives orders, they will not be obeyed" (*Analects*, 13. 6). Yao and Shun were the most ancient of the mythical kings and it was in them that the Tao was most perfectly reflected; yet of Shun Confucius said: "Among those that ruled by inactivity surely Shun may be counted. For what action did he take? He merely placed himself gravely and reverently with his face due south; that was all" (*ibid.*, 15. 4). This means that so deeply was the country imbued with the true Tao that the Emperor had nothing to do: all men simply followed the one simple rule that holds good for all. "Is there any single saying that one can act upon all day and every day?" Confucius was asked; and he replied: "Perhaps the saying about consideration: 'Never do to others what you would not like them to do to you'" (*ibid.*, 15. 23).

## THE CARDINAL VIRTUES

The four cardinal virtues on which the Confucian Tao is based are *jên*, "goodness, benevolence or human-heartedness," which consists in loving others (*ibid.*, 12. 22); *i*, "righteousness, justice"; *li*, "sense of propriety"; and *chih*, "knowledge" or the ability to distinguish right from wrong. These four virtues are in man by nature; they are indeed the Tao peculiar to him as a human being. The only one that needs to be commented on, perhaps, is *li* which has a very wide range of meanings. It means both good manners and the correct observance of the rituals that each man has to perform according to his station in life; it also means modesty and a sense of decency. To these a fifth virtue was added later—*hsin*, "good faith, trustworthiness and loyalty".

It was Confucius' great successor, Mencius, who first established this fourfold rule of conduct. The four virtues are innate in all men, but they have to be developed; it is not enough just to sit back and hope that they will develop of themselves. The doctrine of man's innate goodness is so typical of Confucianism of the early period that we can scarcely do better than quote Mencius himself. This is what he says:

> All men have a certain sympathy towards their fellows. The great monarchs of old had this human sympathy, and it resulted in their government being sympathetic. Having this feeling of sympathy for his fellows, he who acts upon it in governing the Empire will find that his rule can be conducted as it were in the palm of his hand. What I mean by this feeling of sympathy which all men possess is this: If anyone were to see a child falling into a well, he would have a feeling of horror and pity, not because he happened to be an intimate friend of the child's parents, nor because he sought the approbation of his neighbours and friends, nor yet because he feared to be thought inhumane. Looking at the matter in the light of this example, we may say that no man is devoid of a feeling of compassion, nor of a feeling of shame, nor of a feeling of consideration for others, nor of a feeling of plain right and wrong. The feeling of compassion is the origin of human-heartedness; the feeling of shame is the origin of righteousness; the feeling of consideration for others is the origin of good manners (*li*); the feeling of right and wrong is the origin of wisdom (*chih*). The presence of these four elements in man is as natural to him as the possession of his four limbs. Having these four elements within him, the man who says he is powerless to act as he should is doing a grave injury to himself. And the man who says the same of his prince is likewise doing him a grave injury. Let a man but know how to expand and develop these four elements existing in the soul, and his progress becomes as irresistible as a newly kindled fire or a spring that has just burst from the ground. If they can be fully developed, these virtues are strong enough to safeguard all within the Four Seas; if allowed to remain undeveloped, they will not suffice for the service due to one's parents. (*Mencius*, pp. 49–50.)

We shall be returning to the Confucian view of human nature later, for, if man is naturally good, then there must be some explanation as to why he is perpetually backsliding. This unpleasant fact Mencius did not explain.

## THE WILL OF HEAVEN

The first Emperors, Yao and Shun, as we have seen, followed the Tao perfectly. "How great a sovereign was Yao!" exclaims Confucius. "Heaven alone is truly great, but Yao alone could make Heaven his model. How vast his stature! The people could find no words for such a man. Princely indeed was Shun! Majestically he presided over the Empire, yet it seemed nothing to him" (*Mencius*, p. 62).

"Heaven alone is truly great." What is one to understand by these words? There has been much controversy as to whether or not Confucius and Mencius believed in a personal God. If by a personal God we mean the outmoded figure of a bearded old gentleman in the sky recently derided by the Anglican Bishop of Woolwich, then, of course, they did not. If, however, we mean a Being possessed of intelligence and will who orders the paths of the universe, then they most certainly did. In the *Classics*, the *Analects* and the *Book of Mencius* the words "the Will of Heaven" are continually recurring. An alternative word for "Heaven" used in the Classics is *Shang Ti*, the "supreme Ancestor", or *T'ien Ti*, the "heavenly Ancestor": both are used in exactly the same sense, and since both are possessed of will, we might translate either as "God". The Chinese Emperors, then, who styled themselves as "sons of Heaven" might equally well be spoken of as "sons of God". Yet "Heaven alone is truly great", and the supreme virtue of Yao was that he alone approximated his way to the Way of Heaven. In other words he did the will of God so far as lay in his power but acknowledged the unique "greatness" of God.

Essentially the "Will of Heaven" coincides with the moral Tao practised by the philosopher kings; but the Will of Heaven for men does not manifest itself automatically as it does in nature. The sage, if he is worthy of the name, must find it out for himself, and then put it into practice and teach it to others to the best of his ability. This is what Confucius claims to have done:

At fifteen I set my heart upon learning. At thirty, I had planted my feet firm upon the ground. At forty, I no longer suffered from perplexities. At fifty, I knew what were the biddings of Heaven. At sixty, I heard them with docile ear. At seventy, I could follow the dictates of my own heart; for what I desired no longer overstepped the boundaries of right (*Analects*, 2.4).

The Will of Heaven is not simply another word for fate, though its ordinances can certainly not be set at nought by man; it is also a moral power, and so Confucius can cry out in tones of contrition: "Whatsoever I have done amiss, may Heaven exorcize it, may Heaven exorcize it!" (*ibid.*, 6. 26).

Heaven disposes of both life and death, of wealth, rank and moral power, and Confucius confesses that "Heaven begat the moral power that is in me" (*ibid.*, 7. 22). The sage, even if he is a failure on earth (as Confucius was during his lifetime) will be appreciated in Heaven: "The studies of men here below are felt on high, and perhaps after all I am known; not here, but in Heaven" (*ibid.*, 14. 37). Heaven, then, is not indifferent to the lot of man. It asks of him only to follow the Tao of human-heartedness, righteousness, modesty, wisdom and good faith. Yet the Will of Heaven is inscrutable too and transcends by far even the Tao it has ordained for men, and so Confucius says, resigning himself to God's will: "If it is the Will of Heaven that the Way shall prevail, then the Way will prevail. But if it is the Will of Heaven that the Way should perish, then it must needs perish" (*ibid.*, 14. 38).

In *Mencius* Heaven is conceived of in even more personal terms: it is Heaven that raises up or deposes the Emperor, that tests man with suffering, and that can be known even as man knows himself.

Mencius was once asked about the handing over of the Empire by Yao to Shun: "'Is it true that Yao gave the Empire to Shun?' Mencius replied: 'No, the Son of Heaven cannot give the Empire to another.' 'If that is so, when Shun obtained the Empire, who gave it to him?' 'Heaven gave it to him', was the reply. 'When Heaven gave it to him, did it make the charge explicit?' 'No; Heaven does not speak. It merely signified its will through Shun's own conduct and handling of affairs.' 'What are we to understand by that?' 'The Son of Heaven can recommend a man to Heaven, but he cannot make Heaven give that man the Empire. . . . Of old, Yao recommended Shun to Heaven, and Heaven accepted him; he showed him to the people, and the people accepted him. That is why I said that Heaven did not speak, but merely signified its will through Shun's own conduct and handling of affairs'" (*Mencius*, p. 83).

God or Heaven tries men in order to strengthen their characters so that they can develop themselves more fully. "Heaven, when about to charge a man with a great trust, will try his soul with bitterness, subject his bones and sinews to toil and his body to hunger, reduce him to nakedness and want, and bring his enterprises to naught. Thus his mind is made active, his character tempered and his weaknesses are made good" (*ibid.*, p. 106). Thus chastised man comes to know himself as he is, and by knowing himself he comes to know God; for "he who gets to the bottom of his mind comes to know his own nature; knowing his own nature, he also knows Heaven. Preserving one's mind in its integrity and nourishing one's nature is the way to serve Heaven. To practise self-cultivation and await whatever may betide, indifferent whether life be long or short: that is the way to establish one's destiny" (*ibid.*, p. 108).

## HUMAN NATURE

Mencius, as we have seen, considered human nature to be essentially good. He likened it to water which naturally flows downwards; just so does human nature naturally turn to goodness. And just as water can be made to go uphill by violently interfering with it, so can man be deflected from goodness by outside interference. Another Confucian philosopher who slightly postdated Mencius, Hsün Tzŭ, took a diametrically opposite view, maintaining that the nature of man is evil and that any goodness that may accrue to him can only be acquired by training. Man is by nature sensual and acquisitive, and yet, Hsün Tzŭ admits, he is also possessed of intelligence; and intelligence teaches him that in his own interests he must form some sort of social organization with his fellow-men, since in a civilized country where there is already division of labour it is impossible for the individual to "go it alone". Social organization, culture and law, which set a limit to individual acquisitiveness and sensuality, are thus seen to be more in accordance with true self-interest than is the pursuit of self-interest without reference to others, for these others are certain to act in common in self-defence.

Hsün Tzŭ's analysis of human nature was not popular with the later [Neo-]Confucians. They could not, however, deny that human nature included not only intellect, but also acquisitiveness and sensuality. We must, then, they thought, distinguish two natures, an "essential" nature which is in itself wholly good and a "physical" nature (which includes what we would now call the "psyche") which may be good, bad or indifferent, depending on the type of gross or subtle matter of which it is composed. All this is very reminiscent of Thomas Merton's two "selves" and of the dualist conception of man we met with in the Sāṁkhya-Yoga in India (p. 27). Evil comes from the body and from the lower soul which is part and parcel of the body whereas the higher soul is pure *Li*, pure spirit. The mixture of matter and spirit, however, is in the very nature of things—and in this the Neo-Confucians differ radically from the Sāṁkhya-Yogins in India. Man's job is not to separate spirit from matter but so to purify his lower self as to make it a worthy dwelling for the spirit that indwells it.

Neither Confucius nor the Neo-Confucians believed in transmigration, and both were sceptical about life after death ("Till you know about the living, how are you to know about the dead?" Confucius had said (*Analects*, 11. 11)). They did not, then, conceive of man's ultimate goal as being liberation from matter: rather should he perfect in this life the material element which the spirit indwells. The greatest of the Neo-Confucians, Chu Hsi said: "When there is no physical element, even spirit has no home. When the physical element is light and pure, there will be less obscurity and privation. When there is less obscurity, the heavenly spirit will win" (Carsun Chang, *The Development of Neo-Confucian Thought*, p. 268).

Chu Hsi and his predecessors worked out their theory of the two "selves"—the essential and the physical—as a metaphysical counterblast to what seemed to them to be Buddhistic nihilism and in defence of their own tradition which so greatly emphasized the good life that must be led in this world. For them, as for Mencius, the essential man is essentially good: evil comes from the body and the passions that inhabit it. Man's goal is to eliminate the passions as far as possible that he may bring his life into harmony with the universal Tao which is a perfectly articulated whole, a unity that yet has room for diversity.

## TAOISM

Confucianism represents one facet of Chinese religion—the this-worldly, the positive, the yea-saying. Its opposite is Taoism —other-worldly, negative, nay-saying. Like Confucianism, Taoism looks back to a pre-historic paradise, but it looks back beyond the ideal reigns of Yao and Shun to a time when men did not yet feel separate from each other but were merged in a *participation mystique* in which the individual did not distinguish himself from the group. If Confucianism looks back to an age of innocence when Adam, the "All-man", as Blessed Julian of Norwich calls him, was bidden by God to subdue the earth, Taoism looks back to yet an earlier age when the same Adam still lived in harmony with the beasts and birds and had no consciousness of individuality as such. He swam with the current of the mysterious Tao which, though nameless and formless, is yet the source of all that has name and form.

This Tao, however, is not the Tao of Confucius, the Way followed by the philosopher kings of old and itself subject to the Will of Heaven: it is the mysterious source of all things, and to be in tune with it, to let oneself drift along with it, is not only the supreme happiness but the secret of self-fulfilment and of success through apparent failure.

The classics of Taoism are the *Tao Tê Ching* ("The Way and its Power") attributed to the possibly mythical sage Lao Tzǔ who is supposed to have been a younger contemporary of Confucius, and the *Book of Chuang Tzŭ*, a sage who is said to have lived in the fourth and third centuries B.C. The doctrine expounded in these two fascinating books is as elusive as is the doctrine of the Upanishads with which it has much in common. The *Tao*, meaning "Way", reminds one of the Brahman of the Upanishads; like Brahman it is both static and dynamic, ungraspable, indefinable, actionless yet ever active; but in addition it is humble and lowly, like water which naturally tends downwards though, in doing so, the power which it derives from its very lowliness erodes the proudest and mightiest rock.

The Way is like an empty vessel
That yet may be drawn from
Without ever needing to be filled.
It is bottomless; the very progenitor of all things in the world.
In it all sharpness is blunted,
All tangles untied,
All glare tempered,
All dust smoothed.
It is like a deep pool that never dries (*Tai Tê Ching*, 4).

It is "like a bellows in that it is empty, but gives a supply that never fails" (*ibid.*, 5). Like the Indian Brahman once you try to define it you limit it, and if you name it you distort its true nature. Hence it is said:

The Way that can be told is not the Unvarying Way;
The names that can be named are not unvarying names.
It was from the Nameless that Heaven and Earth sprang;
The named is but the mother that rears the ten thousand creatures,
each after its kind.
Truly, "Only he that rids himself forever of desire can see the
Secret Essences" (*ibid.*, 1).

Again, in the following stanzas it would be impossible to say whether what is being discussed is the Chinese Tao or the Indian Brahman:

Such the scope of the All-pervading Power
That it alone can act through the Way.
For the Way is a thing impalpable, incommensurable.

Incommensurable, impalpable,
Yet latent in it are forms.
Impalpable, incommensurable,
Yet within it are entities.
Shadowy it is and dim;
Yet within it there is a force,
A force that though rarefied
Is none the less efficacious (*ibid.*, 21).

The Tao, though the ultimate source of all things, manifests itself in weakness and humility: "In Tao the only motion is returning; the only useful quality, weakness" (*ibid.*, 40). "The power that is most sufficing looks inadequate, the power that stands firmest looks flimsy" (*ibid.*, 41). "It acts without action, does without doing, finds flavour in what is flavourless, can make the small great and the few many" (*ibid.*, 63). And just as the Tao itself conquers simply by being weak and humble, so does the sage by imitating it and doing nothing succeed in all things. "Therefore the sage, in order to be above the people, must speak as though he were lower than the people" (*ibid.*, 66). The sage must make himself the lowest among men that he may be exalted to the highest place, for "the first shall be last and the last shall be first" as we read in our own Scripture: or as the *Tao Tê Ching* says:

Here are my three treasures. Guard and keep them! The first is pity; the second, frugality; the third, refusal to be "foremost of all things under heaven".
For only he that pities is truly able to be brave;
Only he that is frugal is truly able to be profuse.
Only he that refuses to be foremost of all things
Is truly able to become chief of all Ministers (*ibid.*, 67).

## PARADISE LOST

The Taoists and the Confucians have one thing in common: they both look back to a mythical golden age in which complete harmony is said to have reigned on earth. The difference between them, however, lies in the fact that the Confucian sees the moral law of the five relationships and the four (or five) cardinal virtues as the human aspect of the universal Tao, whereas the Taoist regards the very necessity of a moral law as being the first step away from the Tao where there is only effortless activity reflecting the effortless activity of the Tao itself and where there is therefore no need for the conscious practice of virtue. Hence we find the Taoist sages attacking the very virtues on which Confucianism is founded—human-heartedness and righteousness. Confucian moralism is itself an indication that men had begun to be out of step with the Tao:

> Banish wisdom, discard knowledge,
> And the people will be benefited a hundredfold.
> Banish human-heartedness, discard morality (*i*),
> And the people will be dutiful and compassionate.
> Banish skill, discard profit,
> And thieves and robbers will disappear.
> If when these three things are done they find life too plain and
> unadorned,
> Then let them have accessories;
> Give them Simplicity to look at, the Uncarved Block to hold,
> Give them selflessness and fewness of desires (*ibid.*, 19),

The four Confucian virtues each mark a further departure from the Tao: they are wrong because they seek to "name" the "unnameable", to define and pigeon-hole what should be absolutely free.

> After Tao was lost, then came the "power";
> After the "power" was lost, then came human-heartedness.
> After human-heartedness was lost, then came morality.
> After morality was lost, then came ritual.
> Now ritual is the mere husk of loyalty and promise-keeping
> And is indeed the first step towards brawling (*ibid.*, 38).

The *Tao Tê Ching* is relatively moderate in its attack on the Confucian moral code which regards civilization and civilized values as being the human counterpart to the cosmic Tao. The *Book of Chuang Tzŭ*, on the other hand, regards civilization itself as being an affront to and an assault on the Tao itself: it is chipping and hacking at the "uncarved block" of the Tao, a disruption of an original unity and harmony, an outrage against the natural order of things. In the Taoist scheme of things it is original sin. Let us leave the Chinese text to speak for itself:

In the age of perfect virtue men walked along with slow and grave step, and with their looks steadily directed forwards. At that time, on the hills there were no foot-paths, nor excavated passages; on the lakes there were no boats nor dams; all creatures lived in companies; and the places of their settlement were made close to one another. Birds and beasts multiplied to flocks and herds; the grass and trees grew luxuriant and long. In this condition birds and beasts might be led about without feeling the constraint; the nest of the magpie might be climbed to, and peeped into. Yes, in the age of perfect virtue men lived in common with birds and beasts, and were on terms of equality with all creatures, as forming one family; how could they know among themselves the distinctions of superior men and small men? Equally without knowledge, they did not leave [the path of] their natural virtue; equally free from desires, they were in a state of pure simplicity. In that state of pure simplicity, the nature of the people was what it ought to be. But when the sagely men appeared, limping and wheeling about in [the exercise of] human-heartedness, pressing along and standing on tiptoe in the doing of righteousness, then men universally began to be perplexed. [Those sages also] went to excess in their performances of music, and in their gesticulations in the practice of ceremonies, and then men began to be separated from one another. If the raw materials had not been cut and hacked, who could have made a sacrificial vase from them? If the natural jade had not been broken and injured, who could have made the handles of the libation cups from it? If the attributes of the Tao had not been disallowed, how should they have preferred human-heartedness and righteousness? If the instincts of nature had not been departed from, how should ceremonies and music have come into use? If the five colours had not been confused, how should the ornamental figures have been formed? If the five notes had not been confused, how should they have supplemented them by the musical accords? The cutting and the hacking of raw materials to form vessels was the crime of the skilful workmen; the injury done to the characteristics of the Tao in order to practise human-heartedness and righteousness was the error of the sagely men (*Chuang Tzŭ*, 9. 2).

Taoism, particularly in Chuang Tzǔ, is a religion of nostalgia for a long-vanished past, for a past not before Adam fell but before he received the command to subdue the earth, a past when men "lived in common with birds and beasts, and were on terms of equality with all creatures, as forming one family," when "equally free from desires, they were in a state of pure simplicity". Learning and culture are the product of the individualization of the human species when individual men emerge from that condition which precedes self-consciousness in which all is One and One is all, and find, to their horror, that they have become responsible individuals with duties to perform. This inevitable passage of mankind from herd-consciousness to individual consciousness the Confucians accepted and tried to integrate into the total cosmic Tao. The Taoists, on the other hand, preferred to remain children for ever and refused to be separated from their Mother, the Tao, the "Doorway of the Mysterious Female" (*Tao Tê Ching*, 6); and this, as the *Tao Tê Ching* (28) admits, means "returning to the state of infancy".

The Taoism of both the *Tao Tê Ching* and the *Chuang Tzǔ* is permeated through and through with nature mysticism in which, as Tennyson has said, "individuality itself seems to dissolve and fade away into boundless being, and this is not a confused state but the clearest, the surest of the surest, utterly beyond words—where death is an almost laughable impossibility—the loss of personality (if so it were) seeming no extinction, but the only true life".

Confucianism is all about goodness (human-heartedness) and morality (righteousness). While admitting the existence of a supreme directing power which it calls "Heaven" and the need to fall in with its will, it seeks to guide men into the paths of virtue by pointing to a virtuous mythical past—an age of innocence now forever vanished. Its eyes are firmly fixed on this world and man's place in it. Taoism, on the other hand, withdraws from the world, but only because the world of men seems irrevocably to have fallen away from the true Tao; and so all that remains is for the individual to seek to re-integrate himself into the cosmic Tao, thereby isolating himself from his fellow-men. "Therefore I will leave you, and enter the gate of the Unending, to enjoy myself in the fields of the illimitable. I will blend my light with that of the sun and moon, and will endure while heaven and earth endure. If men agree with my views, I will be unconscious of it; if they keep far apart from them, I will be unconscious of it; they may all die, and I will abide alone!" (*Chuang Tzŭ*, 11. 4).

## THE COMING OF BUDDHISM

Taoism is the bridge between the practical genius of the Chinese and the speculative genius of the Indians; and such a bridge was necessary if ever Buddhism was to leave its mark in China. Unlike Hinduism, Buddhism was a missionary religion, and in the first century it made its first inroads into the Celestial Empire. China is probably as suspicious of foreign ideas as any other great civilization, perhaps more so. The success that Buddhism met with in China is then all the more astonishing.

The world-views of the Indians and the Chinese could scarcely be more different. For the Chinese there was no clear distinction between matter and spirit: both were equally real. For the Indians spirit alone was real; matter was at the best an appearance, at the worst an illusion. For the Chinese, man lived but once: for the Indians he was caught up in an endless cycle of rebirth and redeath, escape from which could only be expected after the passage of countless aeons. For the Chinese, man was an inseparable compound of matter and spirit, and when the material element dies they preferred not to speculate on what happened to spirit. For the Buddhists (though not for the majority of the Hindus) what the Chinese called a man was only a perpetually changing mass of perpetually changing atoms; there is no core to him, he is not a person, he is only a "bundle of sensations" with no more reality to him than anything else in the phenomenal world. For the Chinese, both Confucian and Taoist, salvation means integration into the Tao, the cosmic order, whether this includes what man "under Heaven" has added to it or not: for the Indian salvation means liberation from cosmic flux into a state of timeless being. Yet despite all these differences the Buddhists, when they first arrived in China in the first century A.D., found that they had enough in common with the Taoists to be able to enter into a dialogue with them.

The Buddhist world is divided between two main sects, the *Theravāda* (the "School of the Elders"), called by their rivals the *Hīnayāna* (the "Defective Vehicle"), and the *Mahāyāna* (the "Great Vehicle"). There are, however, certain ideas that are common to both schools. The state of liberation which we discussed in the last chapter is usually called "enlightenment", the indispensable virtue that leads to it is detachment, and the arch-enemy that bars the way to it is desire. In addition, both schools of Buddhism fight shy of defining the unconditioned reality experienced in *nirvāna* in any except the vaguest terms. The Mahāyāna likes to call it the "Void" or "emptiness", or simply *tathatā*, "suchness".

When the Buddhists arrived in China they found that the Taoists used terminology similar to their own, and when they started translating their scriptures into Chinese they quite naturally used Taoist terminology. "Push far enough towards the Void, hold fast to Quietness. . . . What has submitted to Fate has become part of the always-so. To know the always-so is to be enlightened" (*Tao Tê Ching*, 16). . . . "It was always and of itself so" (*ibid.*, 51). These are Taoist texts, but they might very well have been Buddhist.

Buddhism became influential in China in the third century A.D. and reached its prime with the advent of the T'ang dynasty in the fourth. In the ninth century, however, Buddhism was officially proscribed, the property of the Buddhist *samgha* (monastic community) was confiscated, and its temples and books were destroyed. From this blow the Buddhists never fully recovered. They did, however, win a covert victory, for the Neo-Confucianism that emerged under the Sung dynasty in the eleventh, twelfth and thirteenth centuries was strongly influenced by Buddhist ideas though they interpreted them along Confucian and Neo-Taoist lines.

Before and during this time of troubles Buddhism had split into a variety of sects, only two of which need detain us here—

the "Pure Land" and the *Ch'an*. The Pure Land we shall speak of later in this chapter as it corresponds in Buddhism to the *bhakti* development in Hinduism. In the development of Neo-Confucian thought, however, Ch'an (Japanese *Zen*) is much more important. Both the Pure Land and the Ch'an sects fared better under the great persecution than did any of the other sects because they depended far less on temples and libraries.

The Mahāyāna (of which the Pure Land and Ch'an are off-shoots) is historically much later than the Theravāda. This the Mahāyānists explain away by saying that their teachings were the secret teachings of the Buddha which had been memorized for centuries by privileged disciples who only committed them to parchment some five hundred years after the Buddha's death. The Ch'an, indeed, though they had scriptures of their own in plenty, nevertheless attached little importance to book-learning, maintaining, as they did, that enlightenment could only come through personal submission to a Ch'an Master who had already experienced it and to whom absolute obedience was due. This direct method is justified in the following verses:

> This is a special transmission which goes beyond the Scriptures,
> There is no use in setting it down in writing,
> Better to appeal directly to the mind of man.
> When one sees one's own nature, Buddhahood will be attained.
>
> (Carsun Chang, *The Development of Neo-Confucian Thought*, pp. 117-8.)

The Mahāyāna in general—and Ch'an is no exception—expresses the idea of unconditioned existence by a word which is usually translated as "emptiness" or the "Void". Typical of the illusive terminology of the sect is a conversation that is alleged to have taken place between the Emperor Wu and Bodhidharma who introduced Ch'an teaching into China in the sixth century. "What is the principle of the Holy Doctrine?" the Emperor asked. "Vast emptiness," Bodhidharma replied, "and there is nothing to be called holy." "Who is it, then, that is now confronting me?" the Emperor asked again, "I do not know," replied the elusive sage.

Ch'an (*Zen*) Buddhism has had a very considerable vogue in

America for some time, and we shall revert to it at the end of this chapter. Its main tenets (so far as it has any) agree with the mainstream of the Mahāyāna. Absolute reality is best referred to as "emptiness" or "suchness"; it has nothing to do with the phenomenal world as normally experienced which is like a kaleidoscope reflecting nothing. Man, that is, the empirical self of Thomas Merton, is devoid of any permanent essence, but the Buddha-nature is everywhere and can be everywhere awakened. Each man is, without knowing it, the indivisible Buddha, but on enlightenment he realizes in a flash that this is so. Fundamentally, however, the Ch'an masters are no more interested in Buddhist philosophy than was the Buddha himself. Even if the human being cannot be said really to exist, you have to behave as if he does since he is at least a potential *locus* of enlightenment. All these ideas were to penetrate into what is called Neo-Confucianism which became the official philosophy of China from the tenth century till the revolution of 1911.

## NEO-CONFUCIANISM

Neo-Confucianism set out to build a synthesis of the Confucianism of Confucius and Mencius, Taoism, and certain aspects of Buddhism. Its grand design was to create a philosophy of religion that would marry time to eternity, this world to the next, man to the One who is at the same time the All. The Buddhists, the Neo-Confucians thought, not without reason, were intent on destroying everything the Confucians held to be valuable—human relationships and the proper ordering of life on earth. "What the Buddhists call 'worldly nets'", said Ch'eng Hao, a Neo-Confucian of the eleventh century,

is the fundamental principle of human relations according to our sages. To get rid of the principle of human relations is the highest point to which the Buddhists aspire. But the fundamental principle of human relations can never be eliminated. The sensations of hearing and seeing; the desires of drinking, eating, and sexuality; and the sentiments of joy, rage, sorrow, and pleasure come from human nature. The Buddhists believe that not until these are done away with can a man attain reality. But I believe that such a way is contrary to reality (Chang, *op. cit.*, p. 204).

Yes, but what is human nature? For in the Confucian tradition itself Mencius had said that human nature was essentially
good while Hsün Tzŭ had said that it was evil. The great Neo-
Confucian, Chu Hsi, as we have seen, cut the Gordian knot and
averred that there are two natures in man, one deriving from
spirit (*Li*) which is essentially good, and the other from matter
which is inherited from the animals and is dominated by the
instincts of sensuality and acquisitiveness. This material element
is morally neutral; depending on its components it may incline
towards spirit or sink down to a purely animal level.

The Chinese words which have been translated as "spirit" and
"matter" are *Li* and *ch'i*. Let us examine a little more closely
what is meant by these words. *Li*, in addition to being spirit, is
also consciousness and reason; it corresponds almost exactly to
what the Greeks called *logos*—the rational principle in the universe which makes things what they are. It is also called the
Supreme Ultimate and has much in common with the Unmoved
Mover of Aristotle. It is also the One proclaimed by the Mahāyāna and the Taoists alike; but it is not the One of Shankara
(p. 48) and his non-dualist Vedāntins, for it does not exclude the
many. As Chu Hsi puts it:

> From the beginning to the end, *Li*, the only reality, is one, but
> millions of things share it in order to acquire essence. Each particu-
> lar thing forms a Supreme Ultimate in itself. Is then the Supreme
> Ultimate divided? The answer is: The Supreme Ultimate is one, but
> each thing shares it so that each thing forms a Supreme Ultimate.
> It is just like the moon which is one, but which is reflected in many
> rivers and lakes and is seen everywhere. One cannot say that the
> moon is split up (Chang, *op. cit.*, p. 257).

*Li*, the Logos, then, is the light that is reflected differently in
every human soul (and this is an idea that we find developed
independently in the Indian tradition too) and this reflected
light is the essential self of each individual man. Man, however,
is an indissoluble compound of *Li* and *ch'i*, of rational spirit and
non-rational matter; and since this is true of man as microcosm,
it must be true of the universe as macrocosm. *Li*, the Logos, is
prior to *ch'i*, matter, in the order of being, though not neces-

sarily in the order of time, for *Li* is by definition timeless. According to Chu Hsi "it is difficult to assert definitely that an order of priority exists between *Li* and *ch'i*. But if one traces back to the origin, one must admit that *Li* is prior. Nevertheless, *Li* is not independent of *ch'i*; rather *Li* inheres in *ch'i*. If there were no *ch'i*, there would be no place for *Li* to stay" (*ibid.*, p. 258). Matter, then, is indwelt by rational spirit, the Logos: it is its *locus*. The two are separable in thought but not in reality. Reality is one, not two; it is a unity in multiplicity, the principle of unity being *Li*, that of multiplicity *ch'i*. *Li* is the immanent God that pervades and indwells the universe. Is it also the transcendent God who directs the universe?

Chu Hsi was asked: "We find the following sentences in the Classics: 'The Lord of Heaven imparts a mind to the people. Heaven assigns a great mission to men. In order to help the people Heaven established kingship. Heaven makes creatures and lifts them up according to their capacities. When they do good, Heaven blesses them. When they do evil, Heaven punishes them.' Does all this signify explicitly or implicitly that in the Empyrean there is a ruler?" Chu Hsi answered: "All this signifies simply that there is reason" (*ibid.*, p. 259). In other words, the universe, since it follows certain rational laws, the marvellous complexity of which modern science is beginning to understand, is itself a rational construction governed by Reason, that is, the Logos.

*Li* is also the Tao in the Confucian sense. Not only is it the living Spirit which controls and indwells the physical world, it also manifests itself in the human sphere as the four cardinal virtues—goodness or human-heartedness, righteousness or morality, modesty which includes decorum and ritual, and wisdom.

Though this is an over-simplification of Chu Hsi's philosophy, it does some justice, it will be hoped, to the synthesis that he and his predecessors were trying to build up. As against the Taoists they asserted categorically that in human society *Li* or the Tao manifests itself supremely in the four cardinal Confucian virtues. The experience of the Taoist mystics, which is the experience of nature mystics of all times and places, is a valid experience. In a mysterious way which cannot be adequately expressed in words, All is One and One is All; "I", the experiencer, wherever I may now be, am yet present everywhere. This experience is thrilling and brings great joy, but it is probably no more than a "biological event" quite divorced from the rational and responsible element in man. The Jesuit paleontologist, Teilhard de Chardin, has described it in these words: "Thanks to the prodigious biological event represented by the discovery of electro-magnetic waves, each individual finds himself henceforth (actively and passively) simultaneously present, over land and sea, in every corner of the earth" (*The Phenomenon of Man*, p. 240). The achievement of the Neo-Confucians was that they harnessed the literally irresponsible mysticism of the Taoists and Ch'an Buddhists to the four cardinal virtues of Confucianism. They had succeeded in constructing a theory of existence in which morality and mysticism were reconciled. Neither is complete without the other, for, as the Taoists saw, the Confucian virtues, once they cease to be spontaneous, become caricatures of themselves. The good or human-hearted man degenerates into a "do-gooder"; righteousness turns sour and becomes self-righteousness; modesty and good manners become a lifeless ritual that has lost all savour; wisdom turns to sophistry. The Neo-Confucians, on the other hand, saw how dangerous it was to turn one's back on self-consciousness which is the unique privilege of the human race in order to recreate within oneself the sense of undifferentiated unity that must have characterized the human race as it emerged from animality; for this meant a refusal to accept responsibility which is the burden as well as the privilege of grown men. The *Tao Tê Ching* (20) had gone so far as to say: "I alone am inert, like a child that has not yet given sign. . . . I alone seem to have lost everything. Mine is indeed the mind of a very idiot." To this the Neo-Confucian answer might well have been: "For Heaven's sake, grow up."

For a thousand years Neo-Confucianism remained the official philosophy of the Chinese Empire: it was China's final word in the philosophy of religion. In the main it is in harmony with the philosophy of the Upanishads in India, but it remained firmly in the realm of nature and showed no craving for a personal God who both indwells and transcends Nature, although it came very near to doing so. The *Li* of Chu Hsi approximates to Aristotle's Unmoved Mover or to Plato's Idea of the Good, but it is not a God that speaks to the heart of man: it is a god of the philosophers, not a living God as Shiva and Vishnu are in India.

## CH'AN OR ZEN BUDDHISM

Buddhism, meanwhile, after its entry into China and its subsequent migration to Japan, transformed itself. Two sects especially developed and flowered despite persecution—the Ch'an (Japanese *Zen*) and the Pure Land.

Zen has, of course, been the subject of innumerable books in the last few decades; and its principal propagandist has been Professor Daisetz Teitaro Suzuki of Kyoto. What Suzuki fails to point out often or clearly enough is that there are, in fact, two schools of Zen, the Rinzai (his own) and the Sōtō. Of these Sōtō is, in fact, the more numerous in Japan, though less sensational. The Rinzai specialize in "sudden enlightenment" and the means they adopt to obtain it in their disciples tend to be violent and bizarre. Unlike most of the other Buddhist sects neither Rinzai nor Sōtō attached much importance to Scripture, and there are stories of Rinzai masters who went so far as to burn copies of the Scriptures as being so much worthless trash, and they would do the same to images of the Buddha. Both sects maintained, in accordance with the mainstream of Mahāyāna philosophy, that the Buddha-nature is omnipresent and that all that mattered was to realize this in oneself here and now. Such realization constituted *nirvāna* which the Japanese call *satori*.

The Zen masters, like the Yogins in India, had mastered the practical technique by which the resistance of the discursive, thinking mind could be broken down so that a state of unconditioned consciousness could supervene; for the greatest obstacle to achieving *satori* is the thinking mind itself. One of the favourite means used to produce this result was for the master to set his disciple an insoluble problem such as "What is the sound of one hand clapping?" or "When your mind is not dwelling on good and evil, what is your original face before you were born?" and so on. The mind worries away at these problems and finally is forced to abdicate, to "let go", and *satori* suddenly supervenes like a flash of lightning. In Suzuki's words: "A penetrating insight is born of the inner depths of the consciousness, as a source of new life has been tapped" (*Essays on Zen Buddhism*, II, p. 84).

The founder of the sect, Bodhidharma, is said to have come to China from India in about A.D. 520. In the ninth century the sect split into two sections, the *Lin-chi* (Japanese *Rinzai*) and the *Ts'ao T'ung* (Japanese *Sōtō*). It was only in the twelfth and thirteenth centuries, however, that the two sects succeeded in establishing themselves in Japan; and here the more moderate Sōtō had a far greater success. It is significant of our times that it is the Rinzai sect as popularized by Suzuki that has been so successful in holding the attention of the American public for many decades; for it concerns itself little with morality, only with the spontaneous achievement of enlightenment and the consequent unleashing of powers hitherto unsuspected and unperceived. The popular American version is admittedly a caricature, but Rinzai too is often a caricature of Buddhism. The founder of the sect himself, I Hsüan, commonly known as Rinzai, is credited by his disciples with the following remarks: "The Buddha is just like other bald-headed monks. Woe unto them who seek enlightenment through him. Seek for your Buddha and he is lost to you." Or odder still on the lips of a Buddhist patriarch: "I hate to hear the name of the Buddha. If you meet the Buddha, slay him, . . . for this is the only way of deliverance."

We have met with this kind of thing before in nineteenth-century India for Rāmakrishna too had said: "With a stern determination I again sat to meditate, and as soon as the gracious form of the Divine Mother appeared before me, I used my discrimination as a sword and with it severed it in two. There remained no more obstruction to my mind, which at once soared beyond the relative plane, and I lost myself in samādhi (trance)."

Sōtō, on the other hand, has received no publicity in America since it offers no short cuts to eternity. Wherever there is serious interest in Zen, however, it will usually be found that the student sooner or later will come to Sōtō though the adepts of this sect have the reticence natural to genuine mysticism.

The sect was introduced into Japan in the thirteenth century by a certain Dōgen, often known by his title, Shōyō Daishi. Dōgen, like the Buddha himself, insisted that morality was the necessary precondition for the attainment of enlightenment. He laid down that his disciples should examine their consciences and confess their sins to the Buddhas (just as the earliest Buddhists had done), to strive for liberation (that is, enlightenment), and to practise the five branches of morality—the giving of alms, gentleness of speech, benevolence in deeds, putting oneself in other people's places, and gratitude All this is to be combined with meditation, and in the end enlightenment will come. Enlightenment, however, does not release one from what the Hindus would call the "bonds" of morality: on the contrary, it must be followed by a yet greater enlightenment in which goodness appears no longer as a duty or an effort, but flows naturally from the enlightened man because he has made contact with the supremely good.

The Rinzai sect regarded the achievement of enlightenment as being everything; and this, they thought, could only be done by submitting to the Zen discipline as it had been developed through the ages under a qualified master. This led them to denigrate the other schools of Buddhism which laid stress not only on meditation but also on the study of the Buddhist scriptures and on prayer. Dōgen, on the other hand, saw good and holy things in all the Buddhist sects, and bade his disciples treat images of the Buddha and the sacred texts with the utmost reverence. These too were stepping-stones leading to the one goal. Yet, though many of the sects had long since deified the Buddha and had indeed peopled the universe with a vast host of Buddhas, the goal of enlightenment is never thought of as union with the Buddha as, in Christian mysticism, the ultimate goal is union with Christ; rather, "to learn the Buddha-way is to learn to know oneself. To learn to know oneself is to forget oneself. To forget oneself means to be enlightened by all the *dharmas*" (H. Dumoulin, *A History of Zen Buddhism*, p. 173).

The older Buddhism had drawn a hard and fast distinction between the world of coming to be and passing away (*saṁsāra*) and the world of timeless Being which they called *nirvāna*. The Mahāyāna, however, made no such distinction: ultimately all things are one in the Buddha. "All being is the Buddha-nature. A part of all being we call 'sentient beings'. Within and without these sentient beings there is the sole being of the Buddha-nature" (*ibid.*, p. 169). To achieve enlightenment means to realize the Buddha-nature within you, and once you have done this you will see the whole external world transformed in the light of this same Buddha-nature that you have discovered in yourself. The Buddha within is the Buddha without—eternal yet operative in time, changeless, yet present in all that changes. The "ego" is forgotten and the "transcendent self" emerges: differentiation is done away with, and all things are seen as they are, indissolubly connected, in perfect harmony, and at one in their eternal ground which is the Buddha-nature.

## *ENLIGHTENMENT*

A Japanese bonze once expressed the nature of *satori* to Fr Heinrich Dumoulin to whose excellent book, *A History of Zen Buddhism*, I am heavily indebted, in these words (p. 275):

> Enlightenment is an overwhelming inner realization which comes suddenly. Man feels himself at once free and strong, exalted and great, in the universe. The breath of the universe vibrates through him. No longer is he merely a small, selfish ego, but rather he is open and transparent, united to all, in unity. Enlightenment is achieved in *zazen* (Zen meditation), but it remains effective in all situations of life. Thus everything in life is meaningful, worthy of thanks, and good—even suffering, sickness, and death. Enlightenment comes in *zazen*, where man becomes completely dedicated to the Buddha. But it does not come through the grace of the Buddha. Indeed, enlightenment does not come from without, but only from within. The self is delivered through its own effort.

We must leave it to the theologians to interpret this type of mystical experience; but surely the *breath* of the universe can only be the Holy Spirit (*spiritus*, breath), the "bringer of life" to all natural things, recognized and seen by that same Spirit who indwells the "temple" of man's body. This is the Spirit manifesting himself as the bond of love and union in the order of nature though not yet as the Spirit of reconciliation between the moral Ruler of the universe (the Father) and morally fallen man.

The experience of satori in Zen Buddhism poses problems to our theologians to which adequate answers have yet to be found. We can only be grateful that it is a Catholic and a Jesuit who has been the first to tackle Zen Buddhism as a historical phenomenon and who has tried to relate it to, and to distinguish it from, the main stream of Christian mysticism. We can also be proud that it was another Jesuit priest, Fr H. M. Enomiya-Lassalle who, attracted by the high seriousness and the dedication of the Sōtō monks he met in Japan, decided to put himself at the disposal of a Sōtō master in order that he too might experience enlightenment. As Sir Charles Eliot has said in his authoritative *Japanese Buddhism* (p. 400): "No one can aspire to be a serious student of Zen unless he at least strives to obtain Enlightenment, and the great difficulty of treating the whole subject is that no one who has not obtained Enlightenment can know what it is and not even those who have obtained it can tell others what it is." Fr Lassalle has both obtained enlightenment and in his little book, *Zen—Weg zur Erleuchtung*, he has told us, to the best of his ability and so far as the subject itself permits, what it is.

According to him there are three stages in the attainment of enlightenment. In preparation for the first the disciple must sit in certain postures traditionally handed down in the Zen sect; he must empty his mind of all ego-centred thoughts, be they good or bad, ambition, envy and fear. The Zen master, who knows by something like telepathy that the disciple is ripe to enter into the first stage, will administer a blow or shout at him at the psychological moment; "and in this way he shocks him out of his darkness. In the pupil's inner being a light arises, just as if a spark were struck from a stone" (p. 19). At this stage the disciple already feels that he "is being freed from something, though he is not quite certain what".

In the second stage the disciple is visited by visions and auditions—in the case of Buddhists by visions of the Buddha, etc. St Teresa of Avila had precisely similar experiences, the visions in her case being of our Lord and his Blessed Mother; but neither she nor the Zen Buddhists nor, for that matter, Rāmakrishna, attached much importance to these phenomena. Fr Lassalle felt himself mysteriously attached to a point at which he was gazing and he saw violet sparks pouring out of each other. This his Zen master interpreted as the liberation of the contents of the unconscious mind; and no Jungian psychologist would quarrel with this. The visions and auditions have no importance in themselves, but if one does not allow oneself to be distracted by them, they leave behind a feeling of "a certain peace like one feels after a good hour of prayer". Moreover, "we cease to be irritated by our fellowmen and we become more pleasant people in the eyes of others".

These two stages, however, are mere beginnings. In the third stage Fr Lassalle felt as if he were being drawn up on high; it was like reaching the top of a mountain and he felt he could stay there indefinitely. To describe his own experience he quotes the words of a Zen master (p. 30) presumably because they correspond most exactly to what he had himself felt.

I was as if dead. Everything was, as it were, cut off. There was no longer any before or after. The object (of my contemplation) and my self had disappeared. The only thing I felt was that my inmost self was wholly at one and filled with everything that is above, below, and round about. A boundless light shone within me. After a while I came to myself again like one who has risen from the dead. My sight, hearing, and speech, my movements and thoughts were quite different from what they had been before. When, gropingly, I tried to think about the realities of the world and take hold of the meaning of the incomprehensible, I understood everything. It seemed to me clear and real. Without wishing to do so I began to throw up my hands and dance with my feet, so overwhelming was my joy. Suddenly I cried out: "A million Sūtras are nothing more than a candle in the light of the sun." How wonderful! How really wonderful!

The actual experience of enlightenment comes suddenly, Fr

Lassalle tells us (p. 31): "All the opposites appear to be transcended. There is no longer any difference between Yes and No. For anyone who has not experienced it, this seems nonsensical; and it must do so. But anyone who has experienced it, knows what is meant." However one may seek to explain it, "it is a real liberation of the human spirit—a liberation from the world of the senses and a liberation from the world of concepts which depends on the senses." Yet, he goes on to say, we are still in the order of nature, though the experience is one of pure Being, of the absolute and unlimited, of the identity of the self with the All and with Nature. Every man can achieve his own enlightenment, for the Buddha-nature is in all by nature; we have only to discover it for ourselves. And enlightenment means "the discovery and activation of a spiritual power which before one neither knew nor had at one's disposal" (*ibid.*, p. 40).

There is no doubt that Fr Lassalle's experience convinced him of the truth of the claims of Zen. Enlightenment releases an unsuspected spiritual power which, one must suppose from the sum-total of the evidence, can be used for good or evil. In the case of the Sōtō monks, with whom he was in contact, it was quite plain that the experience was not only a great joy in itself but also a means to moral perfection and to greater love and understanding of one's fellow-men. It is possible, Fr Lassalle thinks, that this implies a love of God too, though the Sōtō masters never express it in this way, so different is their idea of love from ours, yet he has known cases in which the experience of enlightenment has resulted in faith in God. It is a great pity that he has not told us more about these cases, for the history of Hinduism teaches us that liberation (which is simply another word for "enlightenment") can be the first step on the way to union with God. The Taoist, Neo-Confucian and Zen experiences would appear to represent that initial discovery of the transcendent self which is the first step on the way to union with the living God who, in the *Bhagavad-Gītā* and the whole *bhakti* literature that derives from it, transcends timeless eternity as much as he transcends time and the ever-changing world that is in bondage to time.

## THE TRIUNE BUDDHA

Strangely enough Buddhism which started as an atheistic creed ends in the Mahāyāna by proclaiming the Buddha himself as God. What the *Bhagavad-Gītā* is to Hinduism, the *Lotus of the True Law* is to Buddhism. In the case of the *Bhagavad-Gītā* the ground for the transition from pantheistic monism to monotheism had already been prepared in the later Upanishads; for the *Lotus Sūtra*, however, the transition from the earlier way of thinking is rather more difficult to follow. In the early Buddhist texts the Buddha—Gautama Siddhārtha, known as Shākyamuni, the sage of the Shākya clan—is a man and no more than a man; and no one nowadays doubts his historical reality. Certainly miraculous powers were attributed to him and he is sometimes spoken of as "omniscient", but this means nothing for all "liberated" sages are so spoken of. With the advent of the Mahāyāna, however, all that was to change: the historical Buddha, Gautama, becomes first the God-man and then the godhead itself. This godhead, the Buddha, has three aspects or "bodies"—the Dharma-body, the "body of bliss" and the "construct body". The Dharma-body which can be roughly translated as the "body of eternal law" is the Buddha seen as the Absolute, transcending all things, omnipotent, omniscient, infinite and eternal. The "construct body" is the transcendent Buddha incarnate in Gautama and all the other Buddhas that appear from time to time on this earth and in all the countless worlds with which the Buddhists, anticipating modern astronomy, peopled the immensities of space. The Mahāyāna, however, like the Gnostics of the early Christian centuries, tended to minimize the reality of the celestial Buddha's incarnation and treated it as a mere appearance adopted at will by the Supreme Being for the instruction of men in the true religion and discarded at will when his purpose had been accomplished. The Dharma-body and the "construct" body will therefore be fairly easily understood by Christians: they can, without distortion, be compared to Christ as the eternal Logos and to the Incarnate Jesus as understood by the Gnostics. The "body of bliss", on the other hand, presents some difficulty, but it seems to mean what we would call a "glorious body" in which the Buddhas manifest themselves from time to time.

The three "bodies" of the Buddha have sometimes been compared to the Christian Trinity. The comparison, however, is totally inept. If comparison there must be, it should be to the three aspects of the God-man, Jesus Christ, as he is revealed to us in the Gospel. As Logos he is, in Buddhist terminology, the Dharma-body, as the risen Lord and the Lord who revealed himself at the Transfiguration he is the "body of bliss", and as the child who was born in Bethlehem and died on the Cross he is the "construct body". The parallelism here is striking.

In the Mahāyāna the historical Buddha fades into the background, and a totally new perspective is opened up. No longer are we treading the solid earth, following in the footsteps of the Fully Enlightened One as he tramps the soil of India preaching his message of salvation from suffering to all who have ears to hear. In the Mahāyāna Sūtras (scriptures) we are transported into a heavenly world where Buddhas from all the four corners of the universe meet together in a blaze of glory and light. This is the setting of the *Lotus of the True Law* proclaimed by a transfigured Buddha to an innumerable concourse of Buddhas, Bodhisattvas, gods and men.

## THE BODHISATTVA DOCTRINE

Here we have used for the first time a term which had immense significance in the Mahāyāna—Bodhisattva. Literally the word means a "being of enlightenment". In the early texts it is the term used of the Buddha before he had achieved his enlightenment: it might be translated as "Buddha designate" or "Buddha to be". In the Mahāyāna, however, there is not one Buddha only but myriads of them, and all of them are attended by myriads of Bodhisattvas.

In the Theravāda, the "School of the Elders", as the branch of the early Buddhists with which we are most familiar called themselves, the Buddha was no more than an infallible guide who pointed to the one sure way to *nirvāna*. It was up to the individual to make use of this way certainly, but in the long run he could win through to *nirvāna* only by his own intensive effort. Once he had achieved the goal and entered into his own *nirvāna*, he was known as an *arhant* (literally "worthy") or a *pratyeka-buddha*, a "Buddha in isolation". He had now once and for all done with the world, done with sorrow, suffering, impermanence and its resulting pain. His was now an eternal and timeless form of existence; he was still in the world, but not of it. He had no mandate to teach others since he had achieved the goal and seen the hollowness of all temporal things. A Buddha "in isolation", he could not claim to be a Buddha in the full sense of the word, for these Buddhas, who appear only once in thousands of years, have a teaching mission, while they, the "Buddhas in isolation", are not concerned with teaching.

To the Mahāyānists this seemed a selfish doctrine. They pointed out that this was precisely the temptation to which Gautama Buddha had not yielded. Though he knew better than they that human beings are little more than a bundle of sensations, he nevertheless, fully enlightened though he was, decided to spend the rest of his days preaching his way of deliverance to all sentient beings that had it in them to listen to his saving message. This, the Mahāyānists thought, was the way that they must follow. The true saint is not he who "sits pretty" in his own hard-won *nirvāna*, but he who voluntarily lays aside the *nirvāna* which is already his for the taking, and vows not to enter into his final bliss until he has saved all sentient beings; and so he takes the solemn Bodhisattva vow:

Sentient beings are innumerable: I vow to save them all.
Defilements are inexhaustible: I vow to extinguish them all.
The doctrines of the law cannot be measured: I vow to study them.
The goal of the Buddhas is hard to reach: I vow to attain it.

And so not only do we find celestial Buddhas appearing in vast numbers alongside Gautama, the historical Buddha, but we find too that each Buddha is accompanied by a vast retinue of Bodhisattvas, each and every one of them dedicated to the salvation of all sentient beings. Yet it must always be borne in mind that however much the Buddhas and Bodhisattvas may be multiplied, when all is said and done, they are all really One —one in the Dharma-body which we would call the godhead, separate and glorious manifestations of Him who alone truly IS.

## *THE* LOTUS OF THE TRUE LAW

The *Lotus Sūtra* opens with a concourse of Buddhas, Bodhisattvas, Arhants, gods and men. There is an atmosphere of suppressed excitement, for the transfigured Buddha, Gautama, emits a ray of light from his brow, and this, as all present understand, means that he is about to proclaim some new and unheard-of Gospel. All that he has taught hitherto, he declares, has only been a preparation for what is to come; and the new Gospel is so marvellous that it can only be apprehended by faith. Here there was much murmuring among the Arhants of the old dispensation. What could this be? Had they not already attained *nirvāna*, and had not the Buddha himself repeatedly said that this was the final goal? And so they left the assembly, thinking that they knew all things and that the Buddha, maybe, had taken leave of his senses. The Buddha, however, made no attempt to stop them. "Now, in this congregation," he said, "I am free from twigs and leaves, and have none but the true and real. It is good that men of such overweening haughtiness should have gone away" (W. E. Soothill, *The Lotus of the Wonderful Law*, translated from the Chinese version, p. 68).

This is a direct attack on the Hīnayāna, the "Defective Vehicle", as the Mahāyānists called the "School of the Elders". The Hīnayānists, for their part, regarded the Mahāyāna as an outrageous betrayal of the Buddha's teachings and principles; for the *Lotus Sūtra* goes on to declare with great emphasis and constant restatement that the Hīnayāna ideal of *nirvāna* is a stage on the way only: the goal is to realize the Buddha-wisdom itself, and oneself to become a Buddha. For this faith is necessary, and there is no justification without faith. As has been pointed out time and time again, *nirvāna* in itself is a negation; it is the negation of phenomenal existence, or, as the *Māndūkya* Upanishad puts it: "It causes the phenomenal world to cease." It is timeless bliss, but has no positive content. In the *Lotus Sūtra*, however, the Buddha declares that not only does he will that all men should be saved from this world of pain—this "vale of tears" with which we are all familiar—he wishes too that we should all become Buddhas, "Fully Enlightened Ones", ourselves, "bodies of bliss", shining forth and reflecting the one Body of Eternal Law. He has vowed it from all eternity:

> Of yore I made a vow,
> In desire to cause all creatures
> To rank equally with me (*ibid.*, p. 73).

The *Lotus Sūtra* thus introduces a totally new dimension into Buddhism. The Buddha himself is deified, and as God he denounces the older teaching as being selfish and immature: all sentient beings, in so far as they are beings and not a shifting bundle of sensations, thoughts and emotions, partake of the Buddha-nature and are themselves Buddhas; and to partake of the Buddha-nature means not only to share in the timeless bliss of *nirvāna* but also to have a part in the Buddha's own boundless wisdom, compassion and love. *Nirvāna* itself is an imperfect state; and the astounding insight of the *Lotus Sūtra* is that its author (whoever he was) saw that it is not enough to divest yourself of your lower, empirical self which, as everyone knows, is only too prone to sin.

Even when you have reached *nirvāna*, that is, in the terminology of Thomas Merton and the Hindus, even when you have realized your transcendent self as subsisting in eternity, you are still not free from sin. You will certainly have conquered anger, lust, greed and the delusion that the empirical self is really you, but you are still wide open to the deadliest sin of them all—spiritual pride. Of the Hīnayānists the celestial Buddha said: "The root of sin was deep in them, and their haughty spirit was so enlarged that they imagined they had already attained" (*ibid.*, p. 68).

Why then, the Hīnayānists asked, had the Buddha's earlier teaching insisted that *nirvāna* was the final goal? Why had he lied? We can imagine, indeed, the sensation that the *Lotus Sūtra* must have produced when it first appeared, probably in the first or second century A.D. Here was a work purporting to be the final and definitive teaching of the Buddha which yet seemed to abrogate the older Law. The Mahāyānists contended that this teaching had been given to a chosen few who had transmitted it secretly to their disciples who were only to reveal it when the time was ripe. The strong meat of the new Gospel was more than the infant Buddhist community could digest; and so the Buddha, who was ever "skilled in means", attracted them first with a doctrine that they could understand, granted them the first-fruits of *nirvāna*, only to reveal the full truth later. The Hīnayāna—the "Defective Vehicle"—was then no more than a preparation for the Mahāyāna, the "Great Vehicle". This theme is repeated again and again throughout the *Sūtra*. What the Hīnayānists had understood by *nirvāna* is not the goal at all: it is simply the preliminary stage leading to the goal, for it is quite impossible to share in the Buddha-wisdom as long as you are entangled in the desires and cravings that bind us to this world. *Nirvāna* is certainly liberation from all this, but it is only a rest on the way.

Like Jesus in the synoptic Gospels the Buddha of the *Lotus Sūtra* illustrates his meaning by a series of parables. In one of them he says that once upon a time there was a company of people who had heard of a fabulous Isle of Jewels. They were fortunate enough to have a skilled guide who knew all the snares and pitfalls on the way. But the way was long and tiring. So their guide, in order to reassure and rest them awhile, conjured up a magic city in which they might take their rest.

> So I, [the Buddha says] by expedient methods,
> For their ease preached *nirvāna*, saying:
> "Your sufferings now are ended;
> All your toil is finished!"
> When I knew you had reached *nirvāna*
> And all had become Arhants,
> Then I gathered you together
> And preached to you the real Law (*ibid.*, p. 141).

Again in the parable of the Prodigal Son the same theme is

emphasized, though in this parable we also learn much about the celestial Buddha himself.

Once upon a time a rich man had an only son, but he left his father's house, staying away for many, many years. Fortune, however, did not smile on him, and so in the end he returns to his father's house, sees his father seated in great pomp and luxury, but he does not recognize him. He is overawed by so much splendour and says within himself: "This must be a king or someone of royal rank; it is no place for me to obtain anything for the hire of my labour. I had better go to some poor hamlet, where there is a place for letting out my labour, and food and clothing are easier to get. If I tarry here long I may suffer oppression and forced service." The aged king, meanwhile, had recognized his son, was overjoyed, and sent his servants to fetch him back. They laid hold upon him and would carry him off by force, but the young man, fearing for his life, falls fainting to the ground. His father, seeing this, sends other messengers to him, telling him he is free to do what he will; and the young man goes off to a poor hamlet in search of food and clothing, and he is hired as a scavenger, for which he receives a daily wage. Seeing this, the father has compassion on him, goes to him and wins his confidence, and tells him: "From this time forth you shall be as my own begotten son." So the young man is made the steward of all the rich man's goods; and the rich man, seeing that he is about to die, summons all his attendants and declares to them that the young man is indeed his only-begotten son and that he is the rightful heir to all his boundless wealth. And the interpretation of the parable is that the day's wage the young man received as a scavenger was the *nirvāna* of the "Defective Vehicle", whereas the rich man's wealth was the higher *nirvāna*, the Buddha-wisdom promised by the "Great Vehicle".

In this parable as in the other parables of the *Lotus Sūtra* the celestial Buddha appears in quite a new light: he is a compassionate and loving father, and he is also described as the "Self-existent", a term used by the Hindus to denote the highest deity. The Buddha, then, who claimed to be no more than a guide and a physician to a sick world that knew no God, has now himself

become very God, the "Highest Person". And it is the destiny
of every human being to partake of the Wisdom of this Highest
Person.

But what is this perfect Wisdom that is so immeasurably
superior to the *nirvāna* of the Hīnayānists? Usually it is called
simply *śūnyatā*, "emptiness" or the "Void". This in turn is
described as the "seat" or "throne" of the Buddha, just as his
abode is an abode of love, and his beggar's robe a robe of long-
suffering (H. Kern, *The Saddharma-Pundarîka*, translated from
the original Sanskrit, p. 222). In this passage "emptiness" is
qualified as being "devoid of all *dharmas*", that is, a state that is
unqualified by "things" and which is therefore beyond description.

The fullest description of the Buddha-wisdom, however, is at
the end of chapter V of the *Lotus Sūtra*; and here we see that the
gap between time and eternity, between the transcendent state
of even the highest *nirvāna* of the Great Vehicle and the sublime
virtues that are the ladder by which one reaches it, between the
Buddha's wisdom and the Buddha's compassion, has perhaps
not really been bridged; for after describing the virtues (*dharmas*),
including enlightenment itself, which lead up to the supreme
Wisdom, the author of this wonderful *Sūtra* tells us that all
*dharmas* are devoid of essence as a plaintain is devoid of pith;
they are like magic or a dream. In reality there is neither bondage
nor liberation; nothing really exists except the Buddha's Body
of Eternal Law. "All *dharmas* are the same, all things that are
the same are forever identical (*samasama*). He who knows this,
knows *nirvāna*, deathlessness, and peace (*śivam*)."

And yet so strongly does the *Lotus Sūtra* insist on the im-
measurable difference between the "defective" *nirvāna* of the
"Defective Vehicle" and the perfect *nirvāna* of the Great Vehicle
that we are entitled, perhaps, to interpret this passage in accordance with the general trend of the *Sūtra*, for "emptiness" itself
is reckoned among the *dharmas* that lead to the final *nirvāna* of
the Buddha-wisdom. The author would, then, seem to mean that
in the ultimate "Void" or "emptiness" which is at the same time
the perfection of Wisdom, all virtue, including the supreme

virtues of the Mahāyāna—self-giving, morality, long-suffering, fortitude, contemplation and wisdom itself—exist in an absolute state, rather like the ideas of Plato, at one and identical with the Absolute (for the "Void" being "empty" of all that is relative *is* the Absolute). The Buddhist Void, then, can be likened to our own God who contains in himself all perfections to a superlative degree. In him there is neither defect nor diminution; and this, I think, is true of the Void of the *Lotus Sūtra* if not of the Mahāyāna in general.

The *Lotus Sūtra* marks a turning-point in Buddhism. The Buddha is now no longer a man but the "self-existent" Lord: he is God. *Nirvāna* as understood by the Hīnayāna is no longer the goal: the goal is now to become a Buddha oneself. The Buddhas too have now become innumerable as have their attendant Bodhisattvas and many of them are named. These were slowly to oust the historical Buddha from the unique position he had once enjoyed, and in the *Lotus Sūtra* another Buddha makes a miraculous appearance and such is the awe-inspiring pomp with which he appears that he seems to be greater than Gautama himself.

## THE PURE LAND SECT

One purely mythical Buddha, however, was to captivate the hearts of millions in China and even more in Japan. This was Amitābha or Amitāyush, "Infinite Light" or "Infinite Life". In Japan he is known as Amida, and the cult associated with him has been called in the West "Amidism". In the Mahāyāna the various Buddhas that the Mahāyānists had conjured into life were believed to preside over Buddha-"fields", and it is Amida who presides over the Western Paradise. Billions of years ago he had made the vow that he would not enter into the Buddhahood that was rightfully his in view of the infinite merit he had accumulated in his innumerable incarnations; this merit he would transfer to sentient beings still in bondage to this painful world of space and time who would then enter his Western Paradise known as the Pure Land. Faith in Amitābha or Amida, to use his Japanese name, was enough to win entrance into his paradise,

and this faith expressed itself in the repetition of the formula
*Nama Amida Butsu*, "Homage to Amida Buddha". Repetition
of the formula and the Name, accompanied by a lively faith in
Amida as the Saviour of mankind, was enough to win one
admission into his paradise. It is untrue to say that the Amidists
laid such stress on faith and the reverence of the Name as to
exclude good works, but it did mean that faith in the omni-
potence and infinite mercy of Amida caused his devotees to see
themselves as helpless puppets in his loving hands. If they
sinned, it was because they were impelled thereto by evil deeds
they had done in former lives. Amida knew this and would pardon all, for he wills the salvation of all men; he wills that they
should all enjoy perfect bliss in his company in the Pure Land
where all tears will be wiped away. He knows that the whole Law
inaugurated by Gautama is running down and that men are ever
more prone to sin. So he has made it possible for them, simply
by repeating his Name, to enter into the joys of his Paradise.

Originally Amida's Pure Land was regarded as being only a
stepping-stone on the way to *nirvāna*, but when the cult developed
in its fullness in Japan in the twelfth century, *nirvāna* was forgotten, as was Gautama, the historical Buddha. Thus out of a
religion that had at first recognized no God, and, at least explicitly, no Absolute, there developed, in the fullness of time and
in countries far from its origin, a religion of self-abandoning
faith in the grace of an all-merciful God whom the earthly
Buddha had not even known. This must be almost the strangest
*volte-face* in all the history of religion.

There is, however, this difference between Amidism and the
*Lotus of the True Law*. Amidism regards itself as an easy way for
sinful men who cannot follow the more stringent paths of the
other sects. The *Lotus Sūtra*, on the other hand, sees itself as the
fulfilment of the old "defective" law and as the crown, glory and
summit of the Buddha's teaching, and millions in China and
Japan have reverently and gratefully assented to this claim.

# CHAPTER III

# ISLAM

Hitherto we have been studying the great religions of further Asia, all of which precede the Christian era. It will probably have been noticed that all these Asian religions, as they develop, seem to draw ever nearer to Christianity. This should not surprise us, for it would be strange indeed if God confined his guidance entirely to his chosen people, the Jews, and left the rest of the world in darkness. Cardinal Newman, though he knew very little about the religions of the East, found it impossible to believe that there was any part of the world in which God had not left his impress.

> Now, the phenomenon, admitted on all hands, [he wrote] is this, that a great portion of what is generally received as Christian truth, is in its rudiments or in its separate parts to be found in heathen philosophies and religions. . . . Mr Milman argues from it, "These things are in heathenism, therefore they are not Christian": we, on the contrary, prefer to say, "these things are in Christianity, therefore they are not heathen". That is, we prefer to say, and we think that Scriptures bears us out in saying, that from the beginning the Moral Governor of the world has scattered the seeds of truth far and wide over its extent; that these have variously taken root, and grown up as in the wilderness, wild plants indeed, but living.

This we should have no difficulty in believing, but what are we to say of a religion that sprang up some six hundred years after our Lord's mission on earth, and how are we to explain it?

All the religions we have discussed so far can be classed as in some sense mystical. They tell us a great deal about the dignity and timeless majesty of the human soul, of its capacity to commune and be at one with all created things and with God who indwells both the soul and all that is the work of his hands, but they do not tell us very much about the will of God or his dealings with the human race in space and time. Indeed, the consciousness of eternity tends to make nonsense of the whole process of time: to *be* is what matters; why should we care what goes on in this twilight world of becoming? In the flesh and in this phenomenal world we are the "banished children of Eve, mourning and weeping in this vale of tears"; and the religions of further Asia teach us how to escape from this vale of tears into a realm where every tear will be wiped away and where our exile will be at an end. Time is transcended, and what takes place in this world of space and time can no longer be any concern of ours because it is no more than a dream, or at best a half-real reflection of the eternal world which is our true home. In that world, in which there can be no action because there is no time, there can therefore be no personal responsibility, no "Law" to tell us what we should do and not do; for we have done with doing and are happy only to be. In all the great religions of further Asia this gulf between "doing" and "being" stares us in the face, and these religions themselves were very conscious of the gulf and did their utmost to bridge it; but because they saw that to "be" in eternity was a pearl without price beside which all that happened in space and time was purest dross, they tended to neglect or despise what seemed to them the mechanical processes of the moral law. Witness the contempt of the Taoists for the "good works" of the Confucians.

The danger of mystical religion is that since it is primarily concerned with eternity, not with time, it will treat all that takes place in time and space as being irrelevant; it will pass beyond good and evil. The religion of Israel which is the tree on which the Catholic Church is grafted, is the very reverse of this. For the Hebrews God is not an indwelling spirit but an objective reality of tremendous power, a ruler and a law-giver whose laws must be obeyed. He is the "wholly other" whom man must approach in fear and trembling and to whom he can only say: "I hear and I obey." The Old Testament tells us practically nothing about the divine spark in man which cannot die. Only God is eternal: man is as grass, he springs into life for a brief moment only to wither away.

And the glory of the Lord shall be revealed: and all flesh together shall see, that the mouth of the Lord hath spoken. The voice of one, saying: Cry. And I said: What shall I cry? All flesh is grass, and all the glory thereof as the flower of the field. . . . The grass is withered and the flower is fallen: but the word of our Lord endureth for ever (Isaias 40. 5–8).

Christ, we are told, came to bring us eternal life; he came not only to "fulfil" or complete the Jewish Law, but to deliver us from it. Christianity springs from a Jewish stock, but so different was Jesus Christ from the Messias whom the Jews expected that it is not in the least surprising that they rejected him. Judaism is the prophetic religion *par excellence*, and Christianity sees itself as the fulfilment of Jewish prophecy. In this sense it too is a prophetic religion, but it fulfils the Old Covenant by introducing into it a mystical element which it has in common with the religions of further Asia but which is absent from the Old Testament, for the Old Testament too is a "Defective Vehicle".

## THE CLAIMS OF ISLAM

Some six hundred years after the birth of Christ a new religion arose in Arabia. For the first time in the history of the Semitic peoples a prophet had arisen outside Israel. This prophet was Muhammad who also described himself as the "Apostle or Messenger of God". Islam thus constitutes for Christianity an insoluble problem. It is not difficult to see how the pre-Christian religions can be regarded, each in its own way, as being stepping-stones leading to Christ; but it is not at all easy to see why it should have pleased God to send a prophet *after* he had revealed himself perfectly through the Incarnation of his only-begotten Son.

Islam claims to be the final revelation of God to man. Its Prophet, Muhammad, though an Arab, saw himself as the last in the long line of prophets stretching from Adam through Noah and Moses to Jesus: he was the "Seal of the Prophets" and with him revelation came to an end. He accepted both Judaism and Christianity as true revealed religions—"religions of the Book" —and as such the valid precursors of Islam. Both religions had at their inception been true, but in course of time the true message had been falsified and corrupted by unworthy followers. The truth of Islam was guaranteed by the fact that its holy book, the *Koran*, was directly revealed to God's apostle by God himself speaking through the Angel Gabriel, and these inspired words were recorded on the spot by the Prophet's immediate entourage as and when they were delivered. This was very different from the case of the sacred books of the Christians and Jews which took centuries to assume their final form. It is true that God had revealed himself both in the Jewish and the Christian dispensations, but he had done so through human agency, for the books of the Old and New Testaments have human authors, whereas the Koran has no author but God. Hence when there is a discrepancy between the Koran and the Jewish and Christian scriptures, the version of the Koran must be preferred, for in the Koran God speaks directly and the words recorded there are quite literally the words of God.

At the beginning of his mission Muhammad had believed that the messages he received did no more than confirm the Jewish and Christian Scriptures; and he was therefore baffled when he met with stubborn opposition from the Jews and with sometimes benevolent and sometimes not so benevolent incredulity from the Christians. It is not, then, surprising that in the later parts of the Koran his attitude towards both the earlier religions hardens. He was, moreover, conscious, that there were deep differences between the Jews and the Christians in the matter of "Jesus the Messiah" whom he regarded as his immediate precursor in the prophetic succession. Muhammad had, then, to declare where he stood in this thorny matter; or, as Muslims would say, God was to settle the status of Jesus, so hotly disputed between the Jews and Christians, through the mouth of Muhammad.

It would be no exaggeration to say that, apart from the honour accorded in the Koran to Jesus Christ, Islam is a reaffirmation for the Gentiles of the Jewish Law. For the first time in their history the inhabitants of the Arabian peninsula were told in words of fire that there is no god but God—one, indivisible and holy: "Say: He is God, the One—God, the Eternal. He hath not begotten, nor was he begotten. Never has there been any equal to him" (Koran, 112).

This was probably an attack on Arab paganism rather than on the Christian doctrine of the Holy Trinity, but Muhammad was to deny that doctrine with great vehemence later though he misunderstood it; for the whole message of the Koran is that God is absolutely One and that multiplicity in any form is unthinkable in him. This being the whole burthen of his message, it would be impossible for him to accept the full divinity of "Jesus the Messiah" or to accept the claim made for him by his followers that he was the Son of God.

It is difficult, to say the least of it, for Christians to accept the Muslim claim that in the Koran they possess the very words of God, first because it is not easy to see what God's purpose could have been in sending a prophet, some six hundred years after the Incarnation of his Son, who was to deny or ignore his whole redemptive mission; secondly because, humanly speaking, the contents of the Koran can be paralleled in almost all cases in the Old and New Testaments and the apocryphas ancillary to them. As Muhammad himself knew, there were discrepancies between the two Testaments and the Koran, and these had to be explained. As we have seen he overcame this difficulty by saying that the former books had been corrupted in the course of time, whereas the Koran was directly dictated to him by an angel and must therefore take precedence over the earlier, corrupted, revelations. Given his premisses, this is all reasonable enough, but there are passages in the Koran which seem to admit of no other interpretation than that they are misunderstandings of earlier revelation. The most glaring example of this is the confusion of Mary, the mother of Jesus, and Miriam, the sister of Moses and daughter of Amram in the third *Sūra* (chapter) where the daughter of Amram is said to be the mother of Jesus the Messiah.

## JESUS CHRIST IN THE KORAN

Yet, though it must be difficult, if not impossible, for a Christian to accept that in the Koran are preserved God's own words,

it is not at all impossible to understand how far Muhammad
went towards accepting the mission of Jesus, if not as the actual
Son of God, then at least as the greatest of the prophets before
himself—indeed as greater than himself, if we are to believe what
is said of Jesus in the Koran. Muhammad never claimed to be
more than a man, inspired though he was by the One God to
proclaim the divine unity. Moreover, he was not a worker of
miracles. Jesus, on the other hand, is credited with all manner of
miracles including the raising of the dead "with the permission
of God". Muhammad is Prophet and Apostle, the Seal of the
Prophets, a warner and a herald: Jesus is the Messiah (the
Christ), the Word of God which God cast upon Mary, the Word
of Truth, a Spirit from God, an Apostle and a Prophet of God,
his servant "illustrious in this world and the next". Moreover,
Muhammad is no more than the "Friend of God" whereas
Jesus, in accordance with what is said of him in the Koran, is the
"Spirit of God".

So much concerning the nature of Jesus is conceded in the
Koran: he is the Word of God and his Spirit. It is, then, a little
hard to understand why Muslims do not accept his divinity in
some sense at least. There are, however, passages which emphati-
cally deny that Jesus is either God or the Son of God and these
need careful study. Thus in 5.19 we read:

> Assuredly they have disbelieved who say that Allah (God) is the
> Messiah, son of Mary. Say: Who then will control Allah in the
> least if he wisheth to destroy the Messiah, son of Mary, and his
> mother, and those who are on the earth altogether, seeing that to
> Allah belongs the sovereignty of the heavens and the earth, and
> what is between them? He createth what he willeth; Allah over
> everything hath power.

Here again the purport of the Christian doctrine is simply misunderstood. The Word *Allah* in the Koran corresponds to the
Hebrew *Elohim*, and among the members of the Holy Trinity he
corresponds to God the Father; and Christians have, of course,
never claimed that God the Father is the Messiah. It is the Word
who is the Messiah, and this the Koran explicitly confirms. It is
the idea of sonship that appears outrageous to the Muslims, and

this is often attacked in the Koran: "He hath not begotten, nor was he begotten." Or more violently in *Sūra* 9.30: "The Christians say that the Messiah is the son of Allah; that is what they say with their mouths, conforming to what was formerly said by those who disbelieved. Allah fight them! How they are involved in lies!"

And yet the Koran itself admits that Jesus was born of no earthly father from the immaculate Virgin Mary—from "her who guarded her private parts—so we (God is speaking) breathed into her some of our spirit and made her and her son a sign to the worlds (21.91) . . . and she counted true the words of her Lord and his Books, and became one of the devout" (66.12).

Admittedly to one who was brought up in the atmosphere of pagan Arabia in which daughters were attributed to Allah, the very idea of a Son of God must have appeared obnoxious, for it implied that God who is pure Spirit could have fleshly intercourse with a creature. This, of course, the Christians had never so much as suggested: all that they had said was the Blessed Virgin Mary conceived of the Holy Ghost and that it was therefore legitimate to speak of Jesus in his human as well as in his divine nature as the Son of God. This is equally true of the Koranic passages we have just quoted.

Again, the Virgin Birth is explicitly defended in the Koran against Jewish attack:

> Then [Mary] brought [Jesus] to her people, carrying him. They said: O Mary, thou hast committed a thing improper; O daughter of Aaron, thy father was not a bad man nor was thy mother a harlot. Then she referred [them] to him. They said: How shall we speak to one who is in the cradle, a child? He said: Lo, I am a servant of Allah; he hath bestowed on me the Book, and hath made me a prophet; and hath made me blessed wherever I am, and hath charged me with the prayer and the almsgiving as long as I live; and dutiful towards my mother, nor hath he made me a tyrant, wretched. And peace is upon the day of my birth, and the day of my death, and the day of my being raised up alive (19. 28–34).

In view of the last sentence of this quotation it seems very strange that the whole tradition of Islam rejects the crucifixion and resurrection, particularly as these are explicitly referred to in another passage of the Koran: "Allah said: O Jesus, I purpose to cause thee to die and to raise thee up to myself and to purify thee from whoso hath disbelieved" (3.48). The clear sense of this is again that Jesus died and rose from the dead.

Orthodox Muslim tradition, however, prefers to ignore these two clear passages which plainly refer to the death and resurrection of Jesus, and takes its stand on a passage which is itself obscure. Here (Koran, 4.156) the Jews are reproved for "saying: We killed the Messiah, Jesus, son of Mary, the Messenger of Allah. Yet they did not kill him, nor did they crucify him. . . . In truth they did not kill him, but Allah raised him up to himself, and Allah is sublime, wise."

Even this passage does not contradict the other two. It does not say that Jesus was not killed or crucified, but that the Jews did not kill or crucify him, which is historically and technically true; and in the light of the other two passages it would be reasonable to infer that here too Allah "caused him to die" before he "raised him up to himself". Yet Muslim tradition has it that either another was crucified in his place or that the figure on the cross was a mere phantasm. What is odder still is that the ascension, which the Koran also confirms, was whole-heartedly accepted, and in testimony to this the chapel of the Ascension on the Mount of Olives is to this day in Muslim hands. For them, as for the Christians, Jesus lives on, and in the last days he will return, but the manner of his return is very different for the Muslims from what it is for the Christians. The Muslim tradition has it that in the last days the Messiah, Jesus, will appear in the Holy Land, spear in hand, and having slain Antichrist, he will go up to Jerusalem at the time of the morning prayer. The prayer-leader offers to stand down, but Jesus refuses to lead the prayers and takes his place as a good Muslim behind the prayer-leader in accordance with the custom laid down by Muhammad. Then he will smash the cross to pieces, destroy all churches and synagogues, and slay all Christians who do not accept him as a Muslim prophet. Of all this there is not a word in the Koran.

## THE HOLY TRINITY AND THE KORAN

From all this it will be seen that the gap between the Jesus of Christianity and the Jesus of the Koran is far narrower than the gap between the former and the Jesus of orthodox Muslim tradition. So too in the matter of the Trinity there has been misunderstanding from the beginning. In three passages this most mysterious of all Christian doctrines is roundly condemned, but, as the quotations will show, Muhammad had the strange idea that the third person of the Holy Trinity was not the Holy Spirit but the Blessed Virgin. The passages in which this doctrine is reproved are the following:

> Say not "Three". Refrain, [for it will be] better for you. Allah is only one God; glory be to him; [far from him is] his having a son (4. 169).
> Assuredly they have disbelieved who say: Allah is one of three. There is no god but one God (5. 77).
> [Recall] when Allah said: O Jesus, son of Mary, was it thou who didst say to the people: Take me and my mother as two gods apart from Allah? He replied: Glory be to thee! it is not for me to say what to me is not true; if I did say it, thou knowest it; thou knowest what is in my [inner] self, but I know not what is in thy [inner] self; verily it is thou who art the knower of secret things. I did not say anything to them but what thou didst command me: Serve Allah, my Lord and your Lord. I was a witness over them as long as I remained amongst them, but when thou didst take me to thyself, it was thou who wert the watcher over them, for thou over everything art witness (5. 116–7).

The Trinity, then, so fervently denounced by the Koran, is not the Christian Trinity at all, but a trinity composed of God, Jesus in his human nature, and his mother, Mary. Just how Muhammad came to make so odd a mistake remains a mystery.

Oddly enough there are traces of the true Christian Trinity in the Koran itself. Thus we read: "They ask thee concerning the Spirit. Say: The Spirit is of the *amr* of my Lord; and of knowledge you are given but a little" (17.87).

Now, the word *amr* used here normally means "command", but it has very plausibly been suggested that it here corresponds to the Hebrew *memrā* which itself corresponds to the Greek *logos*, the "Word". This in fact actually portrays the true Christian Trinity—the Lord (Father), the Word (Son), and the Holy Spirit. Again we read: "He sendeth down the angels with the Spirit from his Word (*amr*) to whom he will of his servants, that they may give warning: There is no God but I" (16.2).

The Spirit and the Word testify to the unity of God: they are his witnesses on earth. This too reflects the Catholic doctrine of the Holy Trinity—*qui ex Patre Filioque procedit*. Thus it appears from a careful reading of the Koran itself that the gap between Christianity and Islam as it is first announced in the Koran is very much narrower than the gap between orthodox Christianity and the tradition of orthodox Islam. There is the possibility of dialogue and therefore the possibility of understanding.

It now remains for us briefly to outline the principal doctrines of Islam and to trace their development in history.

## GOD, JUDGEMENT, HEAVEN AND HELL

In the course of time Islam developed creeds much as Christianity did, but they never had the binding force of the Christian creeds. All that is required absolutely of the Muslim is that he should pronounce the *Shahāda*, the "testimony" that proclaims his faith in the One God and his Prophet Muhammad: "I testify that there is no god but Allah and that Muhammad is his Apostle." This is enough to make a man a Muslim. The essence of his faith, however, is contained in the *Fātiha*, the opening chapter of the Koran:

> In the name of God (Allah), the Merciful, the Compassionate.
> Praise belongs to God, Lord of the worlds,
> The Merciful, the Compassionate,
> Wielder of the Day of Judgement.
> Thee do we serve, and on thee do we call for help;
> Guide us on the straight path,
> The path of those upon whom thou hast bestowed good,
> Not [that] of those upon whom anger falls, or those who go astray.

The God of Islam is substantially the God of the Old Testament. He is One and utterly transcendent: he is never referred to as the Father, and men cannot therefore be his "sons" even by adoption. He is absolute Lord, and man is his slave or servant. Nothing is eternal but he, for "everything perishes save his face" (28. 88). He is the living God, self-subsistent, glorious and holy. He is the Merciful, the Compassionate, and this aspect of the divine nature is continually stressed, for practically every *Sūra* of the Koran starts with the words: "In the name of God, the Merciful, the Compassionate." At the same time he is overwhelming Power: he is the Creator, and when he wishes a thing to be, he simply says "Be" and it is. He is the Reckoner, Judge and Avenger, the Bringer of life and death—merciful to believers but fearful in his anger to those who disbelieve.

The vision of the day of judgement which, for Muhammad, as for the early Christians, was expected to come at any moment, possibly in his own lifetime, returns again and again in the Koran like a sombre and awful refrain. It is referred to by various names —the day of judgement, of reckoning, of separation, the encompassing day, the day of standing up and of awakening, or simply the Hour:

So when on the trumpet shall be blown a single blast,
And the earth and the mountains shall be moved, and shattered at a single blow,
Then will happen the thing that is to happen,
The heaven shall be rent asunder, for then it will be weak,
The angels [will be] on its borders, and above them eight shall then bear the throne of thy Lord.
That day ye shall be mustered, not one of you concealed;
As for him who is given his book in his right hand, he will say: "Here, read my book,
Verily I thought that I should meet my account."
He shall be in pleasing life,
In a Garden lofty,
With clusters near:
"Eat and drink with relish, for what ye paid in advance in the days gone by."
But as for him who is given his book in his left hand, he will say: "Oh, would that I had not been given my book,
And had not known my account.

Oh, would that it had been a decisive end!
My wealth has not profited me,
My authority has gone from me."
"Take him and bind him,
Then in hot hell roast him,
Then in a chain of seventy cubits' reach fasten him." (69. 13–32)

The wrath of Allah at the day of judgement and his fierce condemnation of unbelievers is again and again stressed, and even
the righteous must taste of hell for a while: "Not one of you but
shall go down to it—that is for thy Lord a decree, fixed" (19. 72).

The idea of the resurrection of the body which Muhammad
inherited from the Christians seemed as strange and unreason-
able to his contemporaries in Mecca as it does to rationalists
today. For them death was the end, and Muhammad's passionate insistence on the reality of the judgement and the fearful and
eternal pains of hell that were in store for the unbelievers must
have shaken many out of their wonted complacency. Man, however, is not really master of his destiny, for God guides whom he
will and leads astray whom he will; and it is not for man to
question his inscrutable decrees, for God himself has said: "If
we willed, we should cause to come to every soul its guidance;
but true is the saying of mine, 'Assuredly I shall fill Gehenna with
jinn and men together'" (32. 13). Or more terrible still: "We have
created for Gehenna many of the jinn and of mankind; hearts
have they but they understand not with them; eyes have they but
they see not with them; ears have they but they hear not with
them; they are like cattle, nay, they are further astray; these are
the neglectful" (7. 178).

While the unbelievers, the idolaters, the covetous who have
neglected prayer and almsgiving, are condemned to eternal tor-
ment in the fire, all true believers, and particularly the humble,
the charitable, the persecuted, and those who fought "in the way
of Allah", will be welcomed in the gardens of Paradise, the
"Abiding Mansion" and "Dwelling of Peace", "through which
rivers flow". "Verily, those who have believed and wrought the
works of righteousness are the best of Creation. Their recom-
pense is with their Lord—Gardens of Eden through which rivers

flow, in which to abide for ever; Allah will have been satisfied with them, and they with him; that is for him who fears his Lord" (98. 6–8). The essence of the Paradise depicted in the Koran is that it is cool—a garden with plenty of water flowing through it; and this is quite natural when one thinks that Islam arose in a torrid desert in which water not only brought relief but was precious in itself.

Christians and others have not been slow to point out how materialistic the Muslim Paradise is. This the Muslims themselves realized, for when Islam began to develop its own mysticism, the mystic tended to scorn the joys of Paradise which only distracted him from the contemplation of God in whom alone his heart could find peace. For the early Muslims, however, whose faith was simple, and who accepted the words of the Koran in their literal sense, since these were the very words of God, the Gardens of Paradise, with their trees and houris and the promised drafts of wine which the Prophet had forbidden on earth, must have seemed a sufficient reward.

> They are those brought near,
> And are in Gardens of Delight,
> A company from former generations
> And a few from the later;
> Upon couches set with jewels,
> On which they recline facing each other,
> While round them circle boys of persisting youth,
> With goblets and jugs, and a cup of flowing [wine],
> From which they suffer neither headache nor intoxication,
> And with fruit of their own choice,
> And bird's flesh, of what they desire;
> And [maidens] with dark, wide eyes, like pearls treasured—
> A recompense for what they have been doing. . . .
> Mid lotus-trees bent down,
> And acacias thickly grown,
> And shade extended,
> And water outpoured,
> And fruit profuse,
> Not cut off and not forbidden,
> And carpets raised.

Verily we have produced them [the Houris] specially,
And made them virgins,
Loving and of equal age,
For those on the right,
A company from the former generations,
And a company from the later (56. 11–39).

Islam is the religion of the "threat" and the "promise", the
threat of everlasting fire for the wicked and the promise of "Gardens of Delight" for the believer. God is absolute Power, yet
merciful and compassionate; he rewards and punishes whom he
will and as he will, for he is not subject to any law. Man may not
question his judgements, for they are just, however arbitrary
they may seem to man. God is nonetheless ever willing to relent
and to pardon the sinner who repents, but there is one sin which
the Muslims consider unpardonable, and that is *shirk*—associating with God what is other than God, and this includes not only
idolatry but the Christian doctrine of the Holy Trinity. Islam is
the most rigidly monotheistic of all the great religions and the
most zealous in guarding God's absolute unity and transcendence. Between the Creator and his creation there is a gulf fixed
which none may cross.

## SOURCES OF REVELATION

In Islam the Koran, being the *ipsissima verba* of God, is the
primary source of revelation: it is the "Book" *par excellence*, the
words of which, when the meaning is clear, are not open to dispute. There are, however, two secondary sources—the Traditions of the Prophet and the "Consensus of the Faithful". The
"Traditions" are sayings of the Prophet, and from them may be
deduced the *sunnat al-nabī*, the "customs and way of life of the
Prophet", which serve as a model for all good Muslims. In addition there is the "Consensus of the Faithful" which is considered
to have authority second only to the Koran and the Traditions,
for the Prophet is reported as saying: "My community will never
agree on an error." This consensus in fact means the agreement
of a majority of theologians on any given subject, and it has had

the effect of excluding certain questionable doctrines from the field of orthodox belief. It has also adopted doctrines for which there is no authority in the Koran itself.

## SUNNĪ AND SHĪ'A

In the early Muslim centuries Islam was as wracked with theological disputation as was the Christian Church. The earliest schism which plagued the Muslim community and which lasts to this day was that between the *ahl al-sunna*, the "people who followed the traditional practice of the Prophet", generally known as Sunnīs, and the *shī'a 'Alī*, the "party of Alī", who claimed that Alī, the Prophet's cousin and son-in-law, and his successors were the only rightful heirs to the Prophet's succession. The Sunnīs, on the other hand, maintained that the succession or *khilāfa* (Caliphate) was to be settled by popular acclamation, and they therefore recognized the first four Caliphs—the so-called "orthodox" Caliphs, the last of whom was in fact Alī himself— as being valid successors to the Prophet. During this golden age which coincided with the spread of Islam throughout North Africa into Spain, with the overthrow of the Persian Empire and its annexation to the Muslim power, and with the eastward extension of Islam right into Central Asia, Islam was considered to be a theocratic state governed by God through his representative on earth, the Caliph acting as the Prophet's successor. With the murder of Alī, however, and the usurpation of the Caliphate by the Omayyads who made their capital in Damascus, the religious and the secular power, which in the time of the orthodox Caliphs had been inseparable, were divorced, and the Caliph, though he retained the title of "Commander of the Faithful", never regained the religious authority that had once been his.

The Shī'ites, on their side, maintained that the succession had to remain in the family of the Prophet, and this "true" successor they called "Imām" rather than "Caliph". Alī left two sons, Hasan and Hussayn, the first of whom died of consumption. The second, Hussayn, however, rallied what few troops he could muster after the murder of his father against the overwhelming power of the usurper, Mu'āwiyya. The unevenly matched armies met on the field of Kerbelā in modern Iraq. Hussayn was totally defeated, and he himself died a martyr's death, his head being cut off and sent to the Caliph in Damascus. The tragic field of Kerbelā is ever-present to the minds of the Shī'ites even to this day, and they regard a pilgrimage to the tomb of their martyred leader as almost equivalent in merit to a pilgrimage to Mecca itself. Mourning the death of Hussayn, in which the faithful beat and lacerate themselves in atonement for the foul deed of Kerbelā, is the climax of the Shī'ite liturgical year; and extremists among the Shī'a even go so far as to claim divinity on behalf of Alī and Hussayn. Even for the less extreme their intercession at the throne of God is regarded as a sure passport to Paradise and an earnest of salvation.

The Shī'ites themselves split up into sects, but the only one that need detain us here is the most numerous—the "Sect of the Twelve [Imāms]"—which is the official religion of Iran today. According to them the twelfth and last Imām, Al-Mahdī, who disappeared under mysterious circumstances, is, like Jesus, still alive, and will return in the last days to restore the rule of justice on earth when the "party of Alī" will at last triumph over its enemies.

## THE CRYSTALLIZATION OF DOGMA

Just as the early Church dogmas were formulated as and when heresies challenged the traditional teaching, so in Sunnī or "orthodox" Islam were dogmas defined by the "consensus of the people". Only one of the great controversies of the early Muslim centuries need detain us here—the controversy between the orthodox and the Mu'tazilites as they were called, which came to a head in the ninth century A.D. The main points at issue boiled down to three: (i) was God not only infinite Power and infinite Mercy, but also infinite Justice, (ii) had man free will or was he compelled to act as he did by divine decree, and (iii) was the Koran created or uncreated?

The first two questions are really aspects of the same problem. In the Koran it is repeated time and again that God guides whom he will and leads astray whom he will, and yet there are passages like this (4. 44): "Verily Allah doeth not a grain's weight of wrong, and if it is a good deed, he doubleth it, and bestoweth from himself a mighty hire." God, for the Mu'tazilites, was absolutely just; he had made his will clear by his commands and prohibitions in the Koran, and if man were to infringe them, then it was his fault and he would be justly punished. The orthodox, however, considered that to confine God within the limits of human justice was a presumptuous human attempt to circumscribe his absolute power. Not only is the universe the work of the Almighty's hands; every impulse, every motion of the human will is "created" by God. Why, then, are whole classes of human beings sentenced to an eternity of hell-fire, the Mu'-tazilites asked, if their actions are not really their own, but are directly willed by God? Because, the orthodox replied, although God created the will to do an action and the action itself, once this action had been performed, the human being for whom it was decreed, "acquires" it as his own, a singularly feeble piece of sophistry, one would have thought, to justify the doctrine of predestination. Moreover, the orthodox added, however evil a man's life may have been, if he has even a grain of faith left, he will be saved from the torments of hell; for the intercession of the Prophet at the throne of God is very powerful and can save all believers. This is, in fact, a doctrine which cannot be derived from the Koran where no human intercession is said to have any effect at the awful day of judgement.

Similarly with the Koran itself. It was admitted by all that the words of the Koran were dictated to Muhammad by the Angel Gabriel at the behest of God: they are, then, the *ipsissima verba* of God. The Mu'tazilites denied that God's attributes—his power, knowledge, hearing, sight, etc.—were co-eternal with his essence; for this would introduce multiplicity into the One God, and that is *shirk*, the unforgivable sin of associating what is other than God with God. Now, the Koran is the *speech* of God—one of his attributes: it cannot, then, the Mu'tazilites said, be eternal and uncreated. The orthodox, on the other hand, maintained that God's attributes were co-eternal with his essence, and that the Koran was therefore co-eternal with God himself. Thus though we find the doctrine of the Logos of God still applied to Jesus in the Koran, the theologians of the ninth century did not hesitate to transfer it to the Koran; and what they laid down has been accepted as orthodox ever since. As an early confessional formulary puts it: "We confess that the Koran is the speech of Allah, uncreated, his inspiration and revelation, not he, yet not other than he—his real quality, written in copies, recited by tongues, preserved in breasts, yet not residing there" (A. J. Wensinck, *The Muslim Creed*, p. 127).

The complexity of the phraseology and the paradox of the doctrine remind us of the Athanasian Creed. The doctrine is, indeed, almost exactly parallel to the Christian doctrine of the Incarnation, except that in Islam God is made not Man, but Book. *Pace* the "Biblical realists" Islam is the true religion of the Book, the true "biblical" religion, not Christianity.

In the matter of predestination and the uncreated Koran Tradition and the consensus of the faithful might be said to have defined doctrines that were implicit in the Koran, but not unambiguously affirmed. In the matter of predestination the orthodox had to decide between those passages which favoured free will and those which denied it, whereas in the matter of the uncreated Koran they were defending a traditional doctrine on which the Koran was mute. There were, however, other matters on which the Koran gave no clear guidance. For instance, in the after-life would the blessed be able to see their Lord face to face? Tradition answers "Yes", for the Prophet is reported as saying: "When the people of Paradise have entered Paradise, Allah will say to them: 'If you have any desire I will fulfil it.' They will answer: 'Have you not made our faces bright, have you made us enter Paradise, have you not saved us from Hell?' Thereupon Allah will remove the veil and the vision of their Lord will be the most precious of the gifts lavished upon them. Then he recited the verse: 'They who do right shall receive a most excellent reward and a superabundant addition'" (*ibid.*, pp. 63–4).

Similarly in the matter of intercession: the Koran on the whole denies intercession to any human being, but in two passages adds the proviso "except after Allah giveth permission to whom he pleaseth, and consenteth" (53. 27). This was very early taken to refer to Muhammad; it was extended by the Shī'a to Alī, Hussayn and the other Imāms, and in later times powers of intercession were assumed to be exercised by all those saints who had been "canonized" by popular consent. With Al-Ghazālī, who flourished in the eleventh and twelfth centuries, Islamic orthodoxy had reached its definitive form and, despite the efforts of the modernists, it has changed very little since. However, it is not Islam's theological formulations that constitute its strength; this resides first in the stark simplicity of its minimum creed—faith in the One God who reveals himself in the Koran through his Prophet, Muhammad, and secondly in the ritual practices that are obligatory on all believers. These are known as the "Five Pillars of Islam": they are Confession of the Faith ("There is no god but God and Muhammad is his Apostle"), the ritual Prayer, the giving of Alms, the annual Fast, and the Pilgrimage.

## THE FIVE PILLARS OF ISLAM

Muslims are required to pray five times a day, and the ritual, both in word and gesture, follows a rigid pattern designed to emphasize the immense distance that separates man from God. Thus in each of the five prayers the worshipper prostrates himself twice, his forehead touching the ground. The Almsgiving was originally an obligatory contribution for the support of the needy in the community but it has now fallen into disuse. The Fast is still rigorously observed at least in the countryside in Muslim countries. It is far more rigorous than anything the Church has ever imposed, for a pious Muslim may neither eat nor drink nor smoke from sunrise to sunset during Ramadān, the month of the Fast. Since Muslims follow a lunar year, Ramadān rotates in the course of the years throughout all the seasons, and as anyone knows who has lived in the East, to be deprived of water throughout the scorching heat of the day in summer is a very tough penance indeed. At night, however, one may eat and drink as much as one likes.

Of special importance is the Pilgrimage, for more even than

the fixed prayers and the common Fast does the Pilgrimage to Mecca, the Prophet's birthplace and scene of his ultimate triumph, emphasize that Islam is a communal religion—the religion of the "people of Muhammad". Every able-bodied Muslim must, if he can afford it, make the Pilgrimage to Mecca once in his lifetime. The Pilgrimage might be described as the "sacrament of unity" of Islam; it is the Muslim's expression of the unity of all Muslims throughout the world in the faith which has its centre in the holy city of Mecca to which all Muslims, wherever they may be, turn when they perform their ritual prayers. Here, every year in the month of Dhu'l-Hijja, Muslims assemble from all over the world to perform an elaborate ritual in and around the Kaaba, the "House of God", as the great mosque at Mecca is called. The ritual itself with the circumambulation of the Kaaba, the stoning of the Devil, and the sacrifice of camels or sheep is a survival from Pagan times, but the ancient ritual was incorporated by Muhammad into the religion of the one true God: the idols were smashed, and the Pilgrimage henceforth became the visible symbol of the brotherhood of all the "people of Muhammad" under the one God, Creator of heaven and earth, the Merciful, the Compassionate.

Ritual, as we all know, is liable to degenerate into mere formalism, and this had always been a danger in Islam. In addition there is a certain rigidity in Islam which might have paralysed even the tremendous vigour it had shown in that first century of world conquest. Moreover, after the glorious days of the first four orthodox Caliphs had come to an end, the huge empire which the Muslims had conquered infected their pristine faith, except perhaps in Arabia itself, with a worldly spirit—the inevitable price any religion must pay that becomes entangled in the meshes of secular power. It is, then, conceivable that Islam might have died of sheer spiritual inanition, had it not been saved, much against the will of the official theologians and jurists, by a movement which sought to find God not so much in the ritual prayers and the other obligatory duties demanded of all sincere believers as in the inmost recesses of the human heart. This movement is known as Sūfism.

## *SŪFISM*

There has been much dispute about the origins of Sūfism and as to whether it was a purely Islamic phenomenon, or whether it was influenced by Christianity, Hinduism, Buddhism or Neo-Platonism, or all of them. In recent years Christian scholars of great eminence and greater charity have tended to take the view that all the essentials of Sūfism are to be found in the Koran and the Traditions of the Prophet. In this they follow the Sūfīs themselves who, since they were sometimes accused of being crypto-Christians, spared no effort to show that all their teachings which appeared new and revolutionary were in fact to be found in germ in the Koran and the Traditions. The kernel of their teaching was that God is to be found in the human heart and that he is to be sought out and loved as he is in his adorable essence to the exclusion of all created things.

Orthodox Islam, which had first maintained the friendliest relations with the Christians whose lands they had conquered, separated itself ever more widely from orthodox Christianity as and when Islamic dogma became more rigid. The many bridges that were left standing in the Koran itself were allowed to collapse with the passage of time; the Koran itself was elevated to the high dignity of the Word of God made Book over against Jesus Christ, the Word of God made Man. Similarly orthodoxy looked with scant favour on God's great commandment to Israel which Jesus had said contained all the Law and the prophets: "Hear, O Israel: the Lord our God is one Lord. Thou shalt love the Lord thy God with thy whole heart, and with thy whole soul, and with thy whole strength." The first part of this commandment Islam took up with fervid enthusiasm, making it the pivot of its faith. The duty to *love* God, however, which is never clearly enunciated in the Koran, they could not accept, for it smacked to them of presumption. It is impious to compare God to any created thing, for he alone is the Eternal, and "all things perish save his face" (Koran, 28. 88). There can be no communication between the Eternal and the perishable, between Creator and creature. But, the Sūfīs replied, this was not the whole of the story; for just as there were passages in the Koran which implied that man's will was free as against passages which proclaimed that, God's will being wholly untrammelled, he guides whom he will and leads astray whom he will, so were there passages in the Koran which emphasized the nearness of God to man and his love for him. Was he not called *Al-Wudūd*, "the loving"? And did he not say in his Book (3. 29): "If ye love Allah, follow me, and Allah will love you and will forgive you your sins; Allah is forgiving, compassionate"? Was there really a gulf fixed between God and his creatures? If so, how should we interpret these verses from the Holy Book (57. 3)? "He is the First and the Last, the Outward *and the Inward,*" and (50. 15) "We have created man, and we know what his soul whispers within him, *for we are nearer to him than his jugular vein.*" Surely these and similar passages in the Koran justified the Sūfī doctrine that God, though seemingly so remote—so utterly "other"—could yet be loved as the "Inward" who is "nearer to us than our jugular vein".

Again there were generally accepted Traditions which supported the Sūfīs' own inward experiences, for one Tradition declares: "When my servant constantly draws near to me by works of supererogation, then do I love him, and once I have started to love him, I become his eye by which he sees, his ear by which he hears, his tongue by which he speaks, and his hand by which he grasps." And there were many other Traditions not always universally accepted, however, to which the Sūfīs could point to demonstrate the orthodoxy of their views.

Yet there can be no doubt that after the Muslims had overrun Syria and North Africa they unconsciously absorbed many Christian ideas. In the literature of the early Sūfīs we find passages from the New Testament quoted almost verbatim, but their origin is already forgotten, and they are quoted as often as not as being Traditions of the Prophet. Thus we find the parable of the sower in Al-Muhāsibī, one of the earliest Sūfīs, the parable of the wheat and the cockle and the simile of the whited sepulchre in Al-Ghazālī. Al-Ghazālī too reproduces verbatim the great verse of Isaias (64. 4) as restated by St Paul in 1 Corinthians

(2. 9): "Eye hath not seen, nor ear heard: neither hath it entered
into the heart of man, what things God hath prepared for them
that love him."

From the beginning Islam was an extrovert religion and a
communal one: it continued among the Gentiles the tradition of
the Jews. The Muslims, like the Jews, saw themselves as an elect
people, the "people of Muhammad", their Prophet under God,
obeying the Law of God as a people rather than as individuals,
and fighting "in the way of God" against the unbelievers as a
believing people united in the true faith. This left little room for
the pursuit of an interior life, and there is a famous Tradition
which says: "There are no monks in Islam."

Despite all this Sūfism grew, at first unobserved, but later
attracting more and more attention. The early Sūfīs, probably
taking their cue from the Christian desert hermits who preceded
them, would lead a hermit's life, meditating on the mystery of
God's love for the human soul. Later they would associate in
twos or threes, either staying in one place or, more often, pur-
suing the life of wandering friars, begging their bread as they
went. Their aim was to concentrate on God entirely to the exclusion of all created things; and this made them shun human
society as much as possible. In the matter of the observance of
the Muslim Law and its ritual requirements they were scrupu-
lously exact, regarding this as the minimum required by God in
his service. This was only the foundation; and, before the real
religious life could be entered into at all, there had to be a real
conversion of the heart, a turning towards God to the exclusion
of all created things. This could only be accomplished by a total
self-abasement and a total self-surrender to the will of God; and
this meant the mortification of self—the "empirical self", that is,
of which Thomas Merton speaks, or the "animal self" as the
Sūfīs prefer to call it. The conquest of self is the first prerequisite
in the path that leads to union with God. "No one," one of them
wrote, "can attain salvation except by slaying his self in sacrifice
by fasting, long-suffering and gruelling toil." Or again: it must
be "melted by obedience, killed by showing enmity to it, sacri-
ficially slaughtered by despairing of all that is not God, and

murdered by the shame one feels before God". It is the arch-enemy of the true "transcendent self", full of deceit and hypo-crisy, uncleanness and sensuality.

The taming and even the destruction of this lower self is, how-ever, only the prelude to the union of the higher self or soul with God in an ecstasy of mutual love. There are two common words for love in Arabic—*mahabba* and *'ishq*—corresponding roughly to the Greek *agapè* and *eros*, or Latin *caritas* and *amor*—an equal love for all creatures on the one hand, and a passionate and all-consuming love for another on the other. At first the Sūfīs were content to speak only of *mahabba*, for there they were on safe ground, since they had Koranic support for this kind of love between God and man. But when they began to speak of *'ishq*, of passionate love which was accompanied by an insatiate yearning, and leading ultimately to actual intimacy (*uns*) and union, orthodox eyebrows were raised in silent disapproval. This was not the religion of the Prophet that had been handed down to them.

If one is to please God, then one must conform one's character to the "beautiful attributes" of God: only so can one enter into his fellowship and taste the sweetness of his infinite love. How-ever, the early Sūfīs, who considered themselves to be orthodox, always maintained that in the mystic's ascent to God it was always God who took the initiative; the soul had only to wait upon him, relying on his goodness entirely and trusting in it with the trustfulness of a child. This the eighth-century woman mystic, Rābi'a, expressed beautifully in words that condemn even the mystic's total self-dedication to God to the exclusion of all else as still being selfish:

> I have loved thee with two loves, a selfish love and a love that is worthy of thee.
> As for the love which is selfish, therein I occupy myself with thee to the exclusion of all others.
> But in the love which is worthy of thee, thou dost raise the veil that I may see thee.
> Yet is the praise not mine in this or that,
> But the praise is to thee in both that and this.

Whether or not the Sūfīs were influenced by their Christian predecessors in the Near East is largely immaterial. The fact remains that the *type* of mysticism we find among them is well-nigh identical with the Eastern Christian spirituality they found when they first entered Christian lands. Its core is a total self-surrender to God to the exclusion of all else. Like the Christian hermits they had learnt to "love the Lord thy God with thy whole heart, and with thy whole soul, and with thy whole strength", but they had not learnt to love their neighbour as themselves: on the contrary, most of them shunned him like the plague.

By the ninth century the Sūfīs had begun to divide into two factions—those who prided themselves on their orthodoxy and on the "sobriety" of their spirituality, and those who came increasingly to flout the Islamic Law, who prided themselves on their spiritual "drunkenness", and who seemed to have enjoyed shocking their more conventional co-religionists. Despite the fact that the singing of profane songs and dancing had been frowned on by the Prophet and were contrary to the customs and way of life he had left to his people, the more extreme Sūfīs deliberately used song and dance to induce ecstasy and some of them went so far as to deride the obligatory religious practices of Islam. Moreover, so far had they progressed on the mystic path that leads to union with God that they reached a stage in which the purely human personality—the "empirical self"—seemed to be annihilated and replaced entirely by the divine.

It was at this critical stage that there appeared on the scene one Abū Yazīd of Bistām in Eastern Persia. His spiritual master was a man from Sind who appears to have been a convert from Hinduism since Abū Yazīd had to teach him the obligatory practices of Islam in return for which he was initiated into the secrets of "the divine unity and ultimate truths". These "truths" emerge clearly enough from the recorded sayings of this extraordinary man.

In an earlier book, *Hindu and Muslim Mysticism*, I attempted to show that all these sayings, which go far beyond what any Sūfī, however "intoxicated", had ever said before, can be paralleled in the Upanishads and kindred Hindu texts. The inference, then, is that Abū Yazīd had absorbed Hindu or, more specifically, non-dualist Vedāntin ideas without knowing it. It will be remembered that in Hinduism a distinction is made between Brahman, the timeless and impersonal Absolute on the one hand and the creator God on the other, and that while the non-dualist Vedānta made God a mere appearance of Brahman, the later dualist and semi-dualist Vedāntins considered God to be the source of both timeless being (Brahman) and our familiar universe of space and time. Islam, unfortunately, had nothing corresponding to the concept of Brahman—there is only one eternal and timeless Being and that is God, for "all things perish save his face". What then can the mystic say when he suddenly finds that he has, so to speak, fallen altogether out of time into a mode of being where all is One and he can see no manner of difference anywhere? Abū Yazīd did not hesitate to draw what seemed to him the obvious conclusion: he must be identical with God. So, "Glory be to me!" he exclaimed, "How great is my glory !" or in another version of the same, "Glory be to me, I am the Lord Most High!", or again, "Verily I am—there is no God but me, so worship me!"

We have met with all this before in the Hindu tradition and we have seen that the Hindus were able to explain this sense of absolute oneness which is the experience of so many mystics as being not the realization of the identity of the soul with the Absolute, but simply the unfractionable oneness of the "transcendent self" as it exists in the eyes of God in eternity.

It need hardly be said that this and similar utterances of Abū Yazīd caused considerable alarm in orthodox circles, not least among those Sūfīs who still wished to be considered orthodox. The greatest of them, Al-Junayd, to avoid a great scandal, proceeded to write a commentary on the sayings of his outrageous predecessor, and he pointed out, as the Hindu theists had pointed out in similar circumstances, that when Abū Yazīd speaks of "unity", he only *thinks* he has attained to the unity of the godhead; all he has really attained is the "ground of his finite roots", and this is "only a beginning of what might be expected of one who is of the elect".

Al-Junayd, who was perhaps the profoundest mystic Islam ever produced, bearing in mind a tradition (obviously based on Genesis) that Adam was created "in the image of God", saw that if the soul were to realize itself as it eternally is in the eyes of God, it must divest itself of all its purely human attributes, that is, of its "empirical self", and "be as it was before it was": it must realize itself as it is in God's mind. This does not mean, however, that it should for that reason withdraw from the world; for God, though he is eternal in his essence, also operates in time. Man, then, must imitate God in all things: grounded in him in his eternal rest, he must do God's will on earth as well, passively allowing God to act through him. To abandon good works on the ground that in eternity there can be neither good nor evil works since there is neither time nor space without which any action is impossible, is not permissible. "In my opinion," says Al-Junayd, "this is a monstrous doctrine. A fornicator or a thief is better off than people who talk like that." "Those who know God," he goes on to say, "take their works from God and return them to him. Were I to live for a thousand years, I should not abate one jot from the doing of good works unless some insuperable obstacle were put in my way."

Thus Al-Junayd managed to paper over the rift that was beginning to yawn between orthodoxy on the one hand and the more reckless Sūfīs on the other. Even before he died, however, the rift was to be violently re-opened by one whose passion in some ways so closely resembles our Lord's. His name was Al-Hussayn ibn Mansūr al-Hallāj.

## THE PASSION OF AL-HALLĀJ

Until the coming of Al-Hallāj Sūfism had been an esoteric cult, preached behind closed doors to a chosen few. From time to time, indeed, it had come to the attention of the authorities; there had been trials but the Sūfīs had always been acquitted, and no great harm was done. Al-Hallāj, however, quarrelled with the Sūfī brotherhood on this issue of secrecy and proceeded to proclaim the Sūfī message in its most extreme form not only in Iraq but throughout Iran, India and Central Asia. Now, it was

part of the tradition of the Sūfīs that only prophets could perform public miracles; "saints", on the other hand, might indeed
perform miracles but these must necessarily be in private. Al-
Hallāj, however, not only performed public miracles, but was
also accused of putting himself in the place of God, for it was
alleged of him that he had said: "I am the Truth." Whatever Al-
Hallāj's exact mystical theology may have been (and it seems to
have differed but little from that of Al-Junayd), his enemies
seized on this and similar indiscretions and denounced him to the
Caliph. He was arrested in A.D. 921 and lodged in the Caliph's
palace. Here he is said to have cured both the Caliph and his
mother of an intestinal trouble by the laying on of hands. This
brought him high favour with the Caliph for a time, but his
enemies closed in on him, and the Caliph, like Pilate, found himself helpless before them. Like Pilate's wife, the Caliph's mother
intervenes with her son, for she had been warned by her Cham-
berlain: "Be sure," he had said, "that the death of this righteous
man will be on the head of your son." The Caliph, however,
gives way and orders Al-Hallāj to be scourged with a thousand
stripes. After the scourging he was taken from his prison and
escorted to the Baghdad bridge where he was scourged again;
there his hands and feet were cut off and he was hanged upon a
gibbet till he died. After the scourging he is said to have cried
out:

My friend, intending me no harm,
Gave me to drink what he himself drinks, as a host gives a cup to
 his guest.
And when the cup had passed round, he called for the mat and the
 sword.
So must it be for one who drinks with a dragon in summer.

Could he have been thinking of that other crucifixion and the
passing of the cup to the Eleven that prefigured it? Perhaps, but
we cannot know for certain. What we do know is that, like Jesus,
he prayed for his executioners who knew not what they did. After
his hands and feet had been hacked off he cried out: "Look at
these people, thy worshippers; they have assembled here to slay
me, out of zeal for thee, to draw near to thee. Forgive them! If

thou hadst revealed to them what thou hast revealed to me,
they would not have done to me what they have done; and hadst
thou hidden from me what thou hast hidden from them, I would
not be enduring the trial I am now enduring. Praise be to thee
for what thou dost; praise be to thee for what thou wilt."

At this one of the executioners struck him with such force that
his forehead was split; and as he hung mutilated and bleeding
on his cross, he cried out: "Enough for the ecstatic to isolate the
One!", meaning that even on the cross God retained exclusive
possession of his soul so that they could never again be separated.
Following his death, tradition has it, eighty of the leading com-
mon-lawyers of Baghdad signed a deposition saying: "His death
is necessary for the peace of Islam: his blood be upon our heads."

The mysterious resemblance between the passion of Al-Hallāj
and that of Jesus must not blind us to the differences. Christ's
sacrifice fulfilled the Jewish Law in a way that the Jews could not
understand: it was to heal the breach between their nation and
all nations on the one hand, and God on the other, which Adam's
sin had brought about. Al-Hallāj, on the other hand, accepted
the Islamic Law as valid for the people, and the people were
right to crucify him, for he had flouted the Law. He, however,
would have been disloyal to the insights that God had granted
him, to the transformation of his human nature into something
divine that he had operated in him, had he pretended that this
"deification" had not taken place within him. His death, in fact,
solved nothing; for after a brief lull in which the Sūfīs were too
frightened to show themselves, Sūfism continued to advance
until it received the blessing of the great theologian, Al-Ghazālī,
who sought to build a grand synthesis of Islam at its most orthodox and the more advanced forms of Sūfism. How he sought to
achieve this impossible task we have no space to tell; but in the
long run he failed. The tension between the orthodox and the
Sūfīs has never been overcome. There have been periods of
uneasy truce and periods of open hostility, but the basic anta-
gonism between a religion that sees an unbridgeable abyss between Creator and creature and a religion that claims to *know*
that the most intimate union between God and the soul is

possible here and now can never be fully reconciled. In the course of the centuries Sūfism developed very much as monasticism did in Western Europe: Sūfī orders were founded with their houses scattered throughout the Muslim world, and it was they, right up to the beginning of the present century, who, despite many an abuse and much charlatanism, nourished the spiritual life of the Muslim peoples. Now that the Sūfī orders are on the decline and that the various attempts made in the last century to modernize Islam have so far borne little fruit, Islam stands at the crossroads, not knowing which way to take.

# CHAPTER IV

# THE CATHOLIC CHURCH

*O testimonium animae naturaliter Christianae:* "How wonderful is the witness of the soul that is naturally Christian." So Tertullian: and Newman adds in greater detail:

> Now, the phenomenon admitted on all hands is this, that a great portion of what is generally received as Christian truth, is in its rudiments or in its separate parts to be found in the heathen philosophies and religions. . . . Mr Milman argues from it, "These things are in heathenism, therefore they are not Christian": we, on the contrary, prefer to say, "These things are in Christianity, therefore they are not heathen". That is, we prefer to say, and we think that Scripture bears us out in saying, that from the beginning the Moral Governor of the world has scattered the seeds of truth far and wide over its extent; that these have variously taken root, and grown up as in the wilderness, wild plants indeed but living.

The study of the non-Christian religions is sometimes alleged to endanger the faith of the student. This will, of course, depend on the quality of the student's faith. Certainly, if he follows Luther in his extreme hypothesis that original sin *totally* corrupted the nature of man, and that man of himself can do *nothing* to achieve his own salvation, then his faith will, and should be, shaken by his reading of the sacred books of the world religions; for there breathes in them a spirit which is not of this world—a spirit that aspires ever more ardently towards the unknown God "who has made, of one single stock, all the nations that were to dwell over the whole face of the earth. And he has given to each the cycles it was to pass through and the fixed limits of its habitation, leaving them to search for God; would they somehow grope their way towards him? Would they find him? And yet, after all, he is not far from any one of us; it is in him that we live, and move, and have our being; thus, some of your own poets have told us, For indeed, we are his children" (Acts, 17. 26–8).

This being so, it would indeed be surprising if we found nothing in the Eastern religions which did not point to Christ. Before considering what these pointers are, it is essential that we should once again rehearse the cardinal doctrines of our own faith. Unlike the religions of India, Christianity, true to the Judaic stock from which it sprang, sees time not as an unending process, repeating itself ever again from eternity without beginning to eternity without end, but as a straight line with beginning, middle and end. "In the beginning": these are the first words of the Bible, and the last are, "Come, Lord Jesus", looking forward to the end. In the middle is Calvary and the empty tomb. The early Christians mistook the meaning of Christ's resurrection and ascension, in that they thought that the Lord would appear in glory very soon, probably within their lifetime. They had forgotten the parable of the "grain of mustard seed which a man took and sowed in his field; which is the least indeed of all seeds: but when it is grown up, it is greater than all herbs and becometh a tree, so that the birds of the air come and dwell in the branches thereof" (Matt. 13. 31–2). Christ was the seed sown in the tomb of Joseph of Arimathaea, and from the tender plant of the resurrected Lord grew the great tree of his Church which is his body. Christ's earthly mission is not the end: it is the end only of the rule of sin, it is the beginning of the rule of grace.

Many readers of this book will have been puzzled with much that has gone before, particularly with what we have told them about the beliefs of the Hindus and Buddhists. There is so little about God as we understand him, and so much about eternity and timelessness and mystical states of one sort or another, which, wonderful though they no doubt are to those who experience them, seem to have so little to do with our everyday life as we must live it out on earth. All this is true, but we cannot afford to neglect the witness of the Eastern religions, for they emphasize, perhaps too much, an aspect of Catholicism that has been allowed to wither and fade ever since the Reformation wrested our gaze from the God who dwells within us that we might fasten our eyes again on the Judge and Saviour who speaks to us from outside. In so far as we have allowed ourselves to be knocked off that perfect yet precarious balance between the transcendent Lord who is Judge and King and the indwelling Christ we renew in ourselves each time we receive Holy Communion—a balance which it is the Church's mission to preserve—to that extent we have distorted Catholic truth. Orthodox Protestantism killed the great mystical tradition, so much of which had flowered in parts of Europe that were later to fall within the Protestant orbit, and this drying up of the wells of grace that are in the hearts of all of us could not but affect the post-Reformation Church. The condemnation of the Quietists in the eighteenth century finally made all mysticism suspect.

It seems, then, providential that the great mystical traditions of the East should have become known to the West at the very time that its own mystical tradition seemed to be dying out. Could it be that the wisdom of Asia was to be called in to redress the balance of the Church at a time when she was still reeling under the blows of the Reformation?

The Catholic Church has been slow indeed to welcome and acclaim all the truth that any man of good will can descry in the Eastern religions. Long ago we should have been asking ourselves with joy in our hearts: "Will they somehow grope their way towards him? Will they find him?" Why not? Because "after all he is not very far from any of us; it is in him that we live, and move, and have our being." Recently, however, there has been a change for the better. Catholics, guided in this as in so much else that is unexpected and good, by the more adventurous spirits in the Society of Jesus, have come to see how greatly the Eastern techniques of meditation, whether they be Yogin in India or Zen in Japan, can expand and deepen their own Christian life of prayer, for these are the techniques that not only aim at detaching the spirit from its subservience to the body, but which use the body itself to achieve this result. And it is precisely because neither Hinduism nor Buddhism is overburdened with theology that these techniques can be used in the service of any religion or of none. But surely there is danger in this.

There is danger certainly; but only if we mistake the part for the whole, only if we mistake our own soul in its timeless unity for the living God. According to the great Muslim mystic, Al-Junayd of Baghdad, this is not only a danger, but a trap that the Lord himself sets for the mystic who has advanced so far that he has put behind him the *fear* of God—who has forgotten that "it is a fearful thing to fall into the hands of the living God" (Heb. 10. 31). Such a man will mistake his own soul for God, and in every single mystical tradition, whether it be Hindu, Buddhist or Muslim, this will happen; and again in each of these traditions this mistake will be refuted by mystics who have had the two experiences—that of the "isolation" of the transcendent and timeless "self" or soul and that of the overwhelming eruption into that soul of the love of God. The mistake is so easy to make; indeed, it is almost inevitable, for man was made "in the image and likeness of God", and unless he knows God either by faith or, better still, by experience, he can scarcely fail to mistake the image, once purified by asceticism and a total detachment from all temporal things, from the living God whom the image reflects. This "trap" that God sets for the unwary soul the modern Jewish philosopher and mystic, Martin Buber, discerned and warned against in unforgettable words:

Now *from my own unforgettable experience* [he writes] I know well that there is a state in which the bonds of the personal nature of life seem to have fallen away from us and we experience an undivided unity. But I do not know—what the soul willingly imagines and indeed is bound to imagine (mine too once did it)—that in this I had attained to a union with the primal being or the godhead. That is an exaggeration no longer permitted to the responsible understanding. Responsibly—that is, as a man holding his ground before reality— I can elicit from those experiences only that in them *I reached an undifferentiable unity of myself without form or content.* I may call this an original pre-biographical unity and suppose that it is hidden unchanged beneath all biographical change, all development and complication of soul. Nevertheless, in the honest and sober account of the responsible understanding, *this unity is nothing but the unity of this soul of mine,* whose "ground" I have reached, so much so that, beneath all formations and contents, *my spirit has no choice but to understand it as the groundless*. But the basic unity of my own soul is certainly beyond the reach of all the multiplicity it has hitherto received from life, though not in the least beyond individuation, or the multiplicity of all the souls in the world of which it is one—*existing but once, single, unique, irreducible, this creaturely one: one of the human souls and not the "soul of the All"*; a defined and particular being and not "Being"; the creaturely basic unity of a creature (*Between Man and Man*, p. 24).

Buber thus confirms from his own experience what we have already learnt from Thomas Merton about the "two selves"—the "empirical" one of which ordinary people are always conscious and from which evil proceeds, and the "transcendent" one, undifferentiably one, changeless, and therefore "unchanged beneath all biographical change". It is this "self" or soul whose natural habitat lies beyond this world in *nirvāna* and which is always free, always at peace, quite beyond the vicissitudes of time. It is this "self" which, according to the Hindus, is identical with Brahman because, like Brahman, it is eternal. This is what St Paul calls "spirit", distinct from the lower soul or "psyche"; and it is a pity that theologians so rarely bear this distinction in mind.

There are, as we pointed out in the introduction, three types of mysticism. There is what is usually called nature mysticism in which we feel a strange identity with all that is because we see and sense the eternal in all things temporal: "we see the same everywhere". This is what the great Swiss psychologist, C. G. Jung, in his most revealing posthumous autobiography, calls "God's world", a world in which utility has no place because all things there "dwell in a unified cosmos . . . in an eternity where everything is already born and everything has already died". This is the world of Taoism, in which all is one and one is all because there man has not yet arrived at self-consciousness and has not learnt to distinguish himself from his environment and to say "I".

The second type of mysticism is the most strange; it is that described "from his own unforgettable experience" by Buber, and philosophically pin-pointed by the Sāṁkhya-Yoga in India:

the experience of the unfractionable oneness of the transcendent self, separate and isolated not only from the world of matter and mind, but also from all other "selves" and from all present knowledge of the living God. This we meet with among the Sūfīs; it is probably what the Buddhists of the so-called "Defective Vehicle" understand by *nirvāna*. It can be tasted by all men, for this is the "image of God" in the human soul which even Original Sin could not blot out. It is this "image" that the mystic, as Buber saw, is almost bound to mistake for the godhead itself, as the non-dualist Vedāntins did, and as Vivekānanda has done in recent times. It is the "trap" that a jealous God puts in the way of the spiritually proud.

The third and last experience is something quite new: it is the personal encounter of the transcendent self with the living God and the realization of his infinite love. In this encounter the transcendent self itself realizes that the seeming infinity and time-lessness it has learnt to enjoy in itself is as nothing when confronted with the real infinity and majesty of God, even as the poor empirical self, with its worries and cares, joys and sorrows, is as nothing compared to itself. Having given up detachment to all created things that it might "be as it was before it was"—timeless and unsullied—it is suddenly assailed by the fire of the Holy Spirit; and then, as the great Hindu saint, Nāmm'ālvār, steering clear of God's trap into which not a few of his co-religionists had fallen, tells us: "Through cessation of all inclination to other things and the increase of longing for God *in a timeless and spaceless manner*, and through the pangs of separation in not realizing him constantly, he considers himself as a woman, and through the pangs of love loses consciousness." This is the beginning of the soul's love affair with God to which there can be no end.

All this, you may well say, is very interesting, but it seems to have very little to do with Christianity as it is normally understood. True enough: but Christianity itself grows stale from time to time; and each time it loses its savour, something happens to bring back some of the old fervour that launched the infant Church on its triumphant course. In our times it seems that this something became incarnate in good Pope John who reminded us, by simply being his own good self, that all our works and all our faith were as nothing if we lacked the charity to see, acknowledge and welcome the mysterious operation of the Holy Spirit wherever we might find it.

The Church claims to be the new Israel; and, let us make no mistake about it, by making this claim we accept an inheritance of a people whose experience of God has been quite different from the experience of any other race. The Jews *are* a peculiar people simply because they are the chosen people. Others "grope their way towards" God; and God delights to play this game of hide and seek with them (and for the Hindus God's dealings with men are constantly likened to a "game"). But the Jews he chose from all the nations of the earth to be his own people: they alone were granted the terrible privilege of hearkening to the voice of the living God as an awful objective reality who issues commands and prohibitions. In this respect the religion of the Jews stands starkly apart from the great religions of further Asia. These religions appear more "natural", they grow and develop from primitive seeds first into a realization of an ultimate harmony that pervades all things, and secondly into an apprehension of the Author of that harmony whose beauty is reflected both in nature without and in the soul within. Between the utter transcendence of the Jewish God and the total immanence of the Indian God there is a gulf fixed. And so, it would seem, the Church as the second Israel must be for ever closed to the great religions whose way of seeing things is well-nigh incomprehensible to the orthodox Jew. But the Church is not *only* the second Israel: she is also the Church of the Incarnate God who came to make all things one in himself, "reconciling the world unto himself" (2 Cor. 5. 19).

But, the non-Christian may well ask, what need was there for this reconciliation? Do not the religions of further Asia and the mystics of all times and all religions and of no religion at all testify to the oneness of all things and an eternal harmony which, once we *see* it as we should, is still here and now among us? To this we must reply that certainly this harmony is there and per-

vades all created things because all things are what they are
because they are grounded in the Holy Spirit; but because we are
still in time, we fool ourselves if we think that because this harmony can be experienced perhaps once in a lifetime by one in a
hundred human beings, the discord, the misery, and the strife in
which we live are any less real. In any case the harmony the
nature mystics see and feel, and by which they are pervaded, is
only one way of seeing things. Specifically, so far as Eastern
religion is concerned, it is the Chinese way, not the Buddhist
way; and even the Chinese push back this harmony which they
have somehow sensed into a twilight age when self-consciousness
had not yet arisen and when men and beasts still formed one
cohesive family, or into a mythical golden age when men, though
self-conscious, still lived in harmony with the divine law. Nature
mysticism is the experience of the oneness and harmony of all
God's creation as it was before man spoilt it all by growing up,
becoming a responsible individual and, inevitably, falling into
sin. The experiences of nature mysticism, despite the joy and
peace and wonder they bring with them and despite the good
they may do, are nonetheless regressions to a world of innocence
that was shattered when Adam fell.

Of all the Christian doctrines derided by the rationalists the
Fall has perhaps come under the heaviest fire. This seems stupid,
for in practice the acceptance of the doctrine of the Fall means
nothing more than that we recognize that there is something
desperately out of joint both in ourselves and in human society
in general. We may have visions and sensations of a universal
harmony and a universal peace; but there is no harmony, there
is no peace in this world of space and time in which we are compelled to live. The Taoists saw this clearly enough when they
transplanted their paradise back into the morning twilight of
history; and they never claimed that this harmony could be restored in human society as the Confucians vainly tried to do,
though it might be restored in the individual human personality.
A hermit dwelling in the mountains might succeed in re-entering
the mysterious Tao and allow himself to be wafted wherever it
carried him, but human society had shaken itself free from the

Tao and had put in its place its arts and its sciences which necessarily separated it from the mysterious unity of nature which Jung has also called "God's world".

Moreover, the Eastern religions are by no means at one in proclaiming the oneness of all things in the mysterious and nameless Tao. The Buddha saw no such harmony, but only a meaningless and never-ending flux—impermanent, without substance, and therefore painful—a burning house from which at all costs man must be saved. All that is common to the earliest Buddhists and the Taoists is that they both admit that beyond the phenomenal world there is something that never changes, something eternal which man is able to reach; but for the Taoist this something which he calls the "Tao" runs through all nature like a golden thread, whereas for the Buddha it is totally distinct from the turbid flux of phenomenal existence, discontinuous with it, other, and apart. The Taoist would merge himself into the spirit of nature; the Buddhist, on the other hand, seeks final deliverance *from* all natural things and from our human condition itself. If we consider this carefully, we will see that there are two alternative ways of escape from the tyranny imposed on us by Original Sin.

Before the Fall there must have been an age of "original innocence" in which the infant human race, represented by Adam in the Genesis story, walked with God. Man had emerged from the state of group consciousness when, as Chuang Tzǔ puts it, "men lived in common with birds and beasts, and were on terms of equality with all creatures, as forming one family. . . . Equally without knowledge, they did not leave [the path of] their natural virtue; equally free from desires, they were in a state of pure simplicity." These were "the true men of old", who, since they had no consciousness of themselves as individuals, had no fear of death; they were so much part of the group, the "All", that individual death was seen as a mere transformation in which the individual life surrendered itself up without fear or pain or recrimination into the life of the All from which it had become detached for a brief moment.

The true men of old knew nothing of the love of life or the hatred of death. Entrance into life caused them no joy; the exit from it awakened no resistance. Composedly they went and came. They did not forget what their beginning had been, and they did not enquire into what their end would be. They accepted [their life] and rejoiced in it; they forgot [all fear of death] and returned [to their state before life]. Thus there was in them what is called the want of any mind to resist the Tao and all attempts by means of the [merely] human to assist the heavenly. Such were they who are called the true men (*Chuang Tzŭ*, 6. 2).

But at some stage of the evolutionary process "God breathed into his face the breath of life; and man became a living soul" (Gen. 2. 7); he became an individual person, conscious of his surroundings, conscious still no doubt of his mysterious union with all natural things, but conscious too of the presence of the living God who walked with him in the Garden—God, the sole reality, whose being was reflected pre-eminently in his "image", man, as it was to a lesser degree in all things that he had created. This was the state of society which constituted for the Neo-Confucians the ideal, and which they strove, with little success, to reproduce on earth. Every creature that had emerged from the hand of God was perfect in itself, a "supreme ultimate" of its class, reflecting the grand "Supreme Ultimate" who is God.

From the beginning to the end, the Logos, the only reality, is One, but millions of things share it in order to acquire essence. Each particular thing forms a "supreme ultimate" in itself. Is then the Supreme Ultimate divided? The answer is: The Supreme Ultimate is One, but each thing shares it so that each thing forms a "supreme ultimate" [of its own]. It is just like the moon which is one, but which is reflected in many rivers and lakes and is seen everywhere.

Of such was the Paradise of Eden before Adam fell. Not only was there harmony and communion between all created things, and harmony between man and God; there was also harmony and complete integration of all the faculties within man. Being the "image of God", his "transcendent self" turned always towards God and, nourishing itself with God's Spirit, breathed in God's love and transmitted it to the lower soul or ego; and this lower soul, whose business it is to think, decide, and act, thought, decided, and acted in perfect union and harmony with the higher self, God's image, and so with God himself.

With the Fall all this was catastrophically changed. The serpent tempts Eve and she falls; Eve tempts Adam and he too falls. Like any genuinely religious myth the myth of the Fall can be interpreted on many levels. Seen in the light of Far-Eastern religion, however, we can say that Eve here represents the lower soul, for hers is the power of reflection and decision; it is she who "saw that the tree was good to eat, and fair to the eyes, and delightful to behold; and she took of the fruit thereof, and did eat, and gave to her husband who did eat". The lower soul, tempted to "go it alone" independently of God, falls and eats of the sweet fruit that she thinks will bring her independence and power; and she tempts her master, the "transcendent self", who eats too—distractedly, it seems, and without knowing what he does, since the text says nothing beyond the bare fact that he "did eat".

The Fall, then, means primarily the severance of the direct link between God and man—"man" being jointly represented by Adam and Eve who are "one flesh": secondarily, it means that the inner harmony of man himself is upset, for the lower soul, by disobeying the higher and, through the higher, God, stakes its claim to independence. The higher soul or "transcendent self" is now exiled into the unconscious, and most of us pass our whole lives in ignorance of its very existence; and because we do not even know our real self, how are we to know God in whose image and likeness it is made?

After the Fall man is no longer a harmonious whole centred on the transcendent self: he is at war with himself. The centre of the personality has been relegated to the dark recesses of the unconscious, and the "ego", the lower, "empirical self", is at war with itself because it cannot, however hard it tries, get rid of that other self which, even from the darkness of the unconscious, silently reproves it with the still, small voice of conscience; it cannot follow the animal instincts of the body without disquiet and dull remorse because the bond which attaches it to the "other" is exceedingly hard to break.

Man must now live in separation from God, and the whole of the Old Testament is the history of this separation. God is no longer the Friend who walked in the Garden with man; he is the austere ruler who lays down the Law according to which man must live in accordance with God's will and his own best interests. Man, of course, because his lower soul no longer follows the dictates of the higher "self", must perpetually break the Law and suffer the consequences of his pride and self-esteem. This was the glory and the tragedy of the Jews, God's chosen people.

The Gentiles, on the other hand, did not know the Law; but God did not leave them without a testimony still engraved in their hearts, separated from him though they were. He, as it were, scattered clues among them which they were free to follow up and to interpret as best they might. All of them, Jew and Gentile alike, knew that something in man had gone radically wrong, for still they remembered in a confused way the age of innocence in which all had been harmony and all had been one. This hankering after an ideal past dominated the Chinese outlook; the Confucians sought to re-establish the golden age of human-heartedness, righteousness, decorum and wisdom that had been the glory of the just Emperors, Yao and Shun. The Taoists, despairing of human nature itself, sought rather to re-integrate themselves on the purely individual plane into the Tao of nature and the harmony of all natural things. They sought to renew in themselves the age of innocence that was irretrievably lost in the human world around them.

The Indians sized up the situation caused by the Fall differently. Some followed the Taoist path, and sought to merge themselves in the All from which the individual had emerged and into which he must merge again. Others, going beyond this, saw, with a vision unrivalled elsewhere, that what we usually call the soul is not really the centre of our personality at all but merely a mask which hides our inmost being which dwells in eternity and is changeless because it transcends time, space and causation; and, because it does all these things, it shares in the eternity of the changeless principle, Brahman, which they had sensed beyond

the world of change. Salvation, then, meant the discovery of this
timeless being that indwells us, and once it was discovered, then
all the trappings of mortal life had to be struck away, and the
"transcendent self" would then appear in all its brightness, a
single "lamp in a windless place", self-contained, autarchic and
alone. This was to "become Brahman", to enter *nirvāna*, and it
was the ideal of the Sāṁkhya-Yoga among the Hindus as well
as of the early Buddhists.

Christians, when they study Indian mysticism, are frequently
surprised that neither in the Upanishads, nor in the Sāṁkhya-
Yoga, nor yet in early Buddhism is there any mention of love.
Yet if they take the doctrine of the Fall at all seriously, this cannot appear particularly surprising. If man has become separated
from God, he must make the best of his fallen nature on his own
account. God, no doubt, will guide him in this, but he will guide
him in secret and man will be so unconscious of this guidance
that he will attribute it all to himself. The Fall not only separated
man from God, it also relegated the transcendent self to the unconscious where it abides, a pearl of great price, waiting to be
discovered. The Indians did discover it, and once they had discovered it in its timeless peace and unruffled joy they thought
that their journey was at an end. Shaking off the dust of this
transient, imperfect and nasty world, they became what they had
always been from the beginning—Brahman-beings bathed and
dissolved in the boundless peace of *nirvāna*. Beyond this, they
thought, they could not go, because surely this was man's final
resting-place.

From the point of view of fallen man these Hindus and Buddhists were perfectly right. Without divine intervention and divine
revelation man can go no further than to realize the timeless
wonder of his own soul, but such a divine revelation was granted
to the Hindus in the *Bhagavad-Gītā* and to the saints of Southern
India who, while freely recognizing the marvellous beauty and
indestructibility of this transcendent soul or self knew that it
was, even so, dependent on God, and that God, who was its
author, loved it as a father loves his child. This doctrine, which
is central to Christianity, struck the Indian mind with the full

force of revelation, for it flatly contradicted the whole idea of detachment that was of the essence of the teaching of the Buddha, the Sāṁkhya-Yoga, and much of the Upanishads. They had said: Detach yourselves from all that is not eternal so that you may sink into your own eternal essence, aloof from all things worldly even as the lotus flower stands out aloof from the water and mud from which it grew. Now, however, India receives a new and revolutionary message, first enunciated by the incarnate God, Krishna, which says that this detachment is only the prelude to an attachment far more binding than any attachment to the world—an attachment, kindled by love, to the living God who is the source of eternity—of Brahman, as much as he is the source of time. The mystery is how it came about that the *Bhagavad-Gītā* came so soon to be accepted as revelation ranking at least as high as the Upanishads and exercising a far greater influence.

*Vox populi vox Dei.* The saying is not as silly as it might seem. God, in his dealings with the Gentiles, acts more secretly than he did in his dealings with the Jews. The Chinese sage, Mencius, it may be remembered, said: "The Son of Heaven can recommend a man to Heaven, but he cannot make Heaven give that man the Empire. . . . Of old, Yao recommended Shun to Heaven, and Heaven accepted him. That is why I said that Heaven did not speak, but merely signified its will through Shun's own conduct and handling of affairs."

Similarly with the *Gītā*. The *Gītā* does not form part of the Veda, the sacred canon of the Hindus: it is merely a tiny episode in India's huge Epic, the *Mahābhārata*. Unlike the Greek Epics, the *Mahābhārata* contains an enormous section devoted to purely religious topics, yet it is not this that has been "canonized" by the "voice of the people", but the *Bhagavad-Gītā*, the "Lord's Song"—the song of the supreme God, Vishnu, sung by him when he was incarnate on earth as Krishna. Can it be an accident that this little episode in an epic some seven and a half times as long as the Iliad and Odyssey put together, which is itself stuffed with religious teaching, has alone won universal acceptance in India as perhaps the greatest of all the scriptures? Or are we not rather bound to see the mysterious workings of the Holy Spirit preparing us for God's historical Incarnation in Jesus Christ? We see the same thing happening in Buddhism. How was it that the *Lotus of the True Law* which only came to the light of day some six hundred years after the Buddha's passage through this earth, became *the* scripture *par excellence* of millions of Buddhists in China and Japan? It is not enough to say that it filled a spiritual need that earlier Buddhism had left unfulfilled; for this need was filled by the cult of Amitābha (Amida), and the Amidists frankly admitted that their religion was adapted to the popular mind which found it difficult to grasp the idea of *nirvāna*. The *Lotus Sūtra*, on the other hand, rejects the older Buddhism of the "Defective Vehicle" as being but the beginning of the way. It rejects the Hīnayānist view of *nirvāna* as being incomplete, the goal only of the spiritually proud who know nothing of the fatherly love of the celestial Buddha. How was it that this *Sūtra* which denounced the old idea of a personal *nirvāna* as being a mere stage on the way could immediately win general acceptance, unless again the Holy Spirit was making himself heard through the voice of the people? For the *Lotus Sūtra*, while admitting the validity of the Hīnayānists' *nirvāna*, sees it not as the end but only the beginning. Gautama, the earthly Buddha, has been swept aside: he has now become the "self-subsistent Lord" and the loving Father of all sentient beings. The goal is now no longer that men should simply retire into their own timeless essence, but that they should themselves partake of the Buddha-nature, the essence of which is transcendent Wisdom and infinite Compassion. In this marvellous *Sūtra* the historical Buddha is in the process of being transformed into the God-man Christ. Both the *Gītā* and the *Lotus Sūtra* agree in this, that the realization of one's own soul is but the beginning of the way; both agree that it is love that brings the soul into the presence of the unknown God. Asia had thus been well prepared for the hearing of the good news that God had actually become man in history in the person of Jesus Christ.

They had been well prepared, it is true; but one thing was lacking as it was lacking in the Jewish preparation, at least as the

Jews, forgetting the Suffering Servant of Isaias, interpreted it. They had thought—and who can blame them?—that when the Messiah came, he would come as a glorious king or at least born into a family of kings as was Krishna in the Indian myth and the Buddha in Indian history. This time it is China which bears witness to the "weakness of God" that is yet "stronger than men".

The Tao, it will be remembered, which is the unnamed source of all things and the "power" in all things, has "only one useful quality", and that is "weakness"; its "most sufficing" power "looks" inadequate, and this power "that [really] stands firmest looks flimsy". "It acts without action, does without doing, finds flavour in what is flavourless, can make the small great and the few many." And just as the Tao conquers by being weak, so does the sage who incarnates the Tao achieve his object by making himself the lowest of the low. "Therefore the sage, in order to be above the people, must speak as if he were lower than the people." Is it, then, surprising that the Tao, the Logos, incarnate should have "humbled himself, becoming obedient unto death, even to the death of the cross; for which cause, God also hath exalted him and hath given him a name which is above all names: that in the name of Jesus every knee should bow, of those that are in heaven, on earth, and under the earth" (Phil. 2. 8–10). For, in the beginning, it will be remembered:

> The Way that can be told is not the Unvarying Way;
> The names that can be named are not the unvarying names.
> It was from the Nameless that Heaven and Earth sprang;
> The named is but the mother that rears the ten thousand creatures,
>     each after its kind.

The Tao became flesh, and the Nameless received a name: "His name shall be Jesus."

Christ said that he came not to destroy the Law and the prophets but to fulfil them; and if this is true of the Law and the prophets of Israel, it is equally true of the "law and the prophets" of India and China. It was India that familiarized the world with the idea of an incarnate God, and it was China which, in the *Tai*

*Tê Ching*, showed what sort of God he was and what would be the manner of his coming; but the true purpose of the coming of Christ can only be seen as a joint fulfilment of the aspirations of Jew and Gentile alike.

In the *Bhagavad-Gītā* God appears incarnate as Krishna who preaches the new doctrine of God's love for man and man's answering love to God, and once he has pointed the way to the living God who stood as high above the changeless and timeless Brahman as Brahman stood above the "empirical self" and the world in which it moves, India has demanded to know what that God is like. Oddly enough, the Krishna of the *bhakti* cults is not the Krishna of the Great Epic who is the mouthpiece of the *Bhagavad-Gītā*, for *this* Krishna all too often resorts to tricks and dubious stratagems to attain his ends, and this aspect of him was quickly forgotten. The Krishna of the *bhakti* cults, however, is a wayward boy who beguiles the cowherds' daughters with the sweet piping of his flute, and for the Hindus this represents God's wooing of the human soul and the soul's ecstatic response to the divine call. Gone is the terrible aspect of God which, in its grand theophany, the *Gītā* had revealed. The picture is too sugary, for any true picture of God must make room for his terrible justice as well as for his gracious mercy, as Islam teaches us. And it is for this reason that the Krishna of the Epic rings more true, for in him there is tragedy and pathos. It had been his mission as incarnate God to re-establish the rule of righteousness on earth; and he did so, though at a terrible cost. Once he had re-established Yudhishthira, the King of Righteousness, on his throne, he returned home only to meet with a tragic and humiliating death. Deserted by his own tribe who tear themselves to pieces in a drunken orgy, he retires to the sea-shore to meditate, and is there slain by a fowler who mistakes him for a gazelle. Only by suffering failure and humiliation and by being slain like an animal can he ascend into heaven and enter into his glory. Does this not prefigure in a strange way the incomprehensible humiliation of the Cross?

The *Bhagavad-Gītā* and the *Lotus Sūtra* both announce the glad tidings that man's true destiny is not to enjoy forever that fragment of eternity which even the Fall could not take away from him, but rather to bestir himself once again, leaving behind this eternal but still "defective" rest in order that he may be at one with his Lord. God became man in the person of Jesus Christ in order that the "unknown" God, imperfectly adumbrated in the figure of Krishna and, more graphically though still not perfectly, in the terrifying yet adorable figure of Shiva, might be known. Christ, as perfect man, has not only an "empirical" soul and a body, but also a "transcendent self". Now, the Hīnayāna Buddhists and the Hindus who followed them largely in this, had taught that this "self", because it abides in eternity, must transcend all the opposites, including good and evil: it has passed beyond what the Chinese call *chih*, the "wisdom" that distinguishes between right and wrong; for being outside time it cannot act and therefore cannot sin. The *Lotus Sūtra*, however, pointed out that the most insidious sin of all was still wide open to it—spiritual pride—the belief that the transcendent self alone can reach the highest goal than which, it thinks, no higher goal can be attained.

Experience tells us that, as Martin Buber has so forcefully pointed out, the soul of man, once it has realized its immortal and timeless "ground", thinks and must think that it has attained the "groundless" godhead itself. God, then, must become man both to show man his true nature which is a self-giving love which does not shrink from laying down its life for its friends, and to show him that this "transcendent self" too must be crucified and immolated along with the empirical self, the necessity for whose taming and subjection had been self-evident to the Indian mind. It must be crucified in order that the spiritual pride of self-sufficiency may be once and for all burnt out, and that it may thus ascend into heaven to be united forever with the Father in the love which is the Holy Spirit through the self-immolation of the Incarnate Word, its own perfect exemplar.

Christ's mission was to bring together all things that had been separated by sin. First he must make the human being whole himself, for only then can he offer him back to the Father in the same perfection in which he was made. Christ, the second Adam, is crucified that the first Adam, living on in his children as their "transcendent self", may be crucified with him, die to pride, and resurrect in perfect charity. The inner Eve, too—the "empirical" soul—must be re-integrated into her redeemed consort, the transcendent self, and through him into Christ and God. The Buddha's original doctrine is turned upside down, even more than it was in the *Lotus Sūtra*; for the Buddha came to deliver spirit from the toils of matter, Christ came to sanctify man and through man all the material world. The gap between the spiritual and the material caused by original sin which left man no alternative but to concentrate on the spiritual, as the Buddha rightly saw, was to be closed, and matter was to be pressed into the service of spirit so that the harmony of the universe which the Chinese, above all others, so keenly sensed, might be restored —and restored on a higher because a morally responsible plane in which the virtues of human-heartedness, righteousness, decorum and wisdom could flourish in the light of the Holy Spirit, the "Lord and Giver of Life", who is at the same time love.

Christ came not to destroy but to fulfil all the insights into the nature of divine truth that God had scattered throughout the world to guide men in their return to him out of this "valley of tears". And in these latter days, to counteract, perhaps, the monistic reaction of Vivekānanda and others in India who once again proclaimed their identity with the Absolute, he sent Mahatma Gandhi to remind the Hindus that God was not only Being, Logos and Bliss, but also "Truth and Love", "ethics and morality", and last but not least "conscience".

*O testimonium animae naturaliter Christianae.* It seems to be indeed true that all man's highest aspirations in the further East as in Jewry point with increasing urgency to the Incarnation of the Righteous and Loving God. And the sad fact that these very Asians have not taken him to themselves whole-heartedly is due to the equally sad fact that they have seen little of him but a shabby caricature. As Simone Weil has pointed out, it is easy to accept that the Catholic Church is *de jure* the one human organization that can claim the allegiance of all mankind because in the

Person of Jesus and the Church he founded are fulfilled both the inspired insights of the Hindus and Mahāyāna Buddhists which point to the potential deification of all human beings in the all-embracing love of the one God, and the social ideal of the Neo-Confucianists which envisaged a harmonious society of perfected beings under the sway of the One Supreme Ultimate; but it remains horribly true that the Church, though it lives by the breath of the Holy Spirit and is nourished by the Body and Blood of Christ, nevertheless is still wracked and riddled with human sin. It has a history of bloodshed, persecution, and bigotry behind it which it is only now beginning to live down thanks to the wide "human-heartedness" that radiated from the heart of Pope John XXIII.

"By their fruits shall ye know them", our Lord said; and some of our fruits in the past have been bitter, rotten fruits that would, had it been possible, have corrupted the very tree, Christ, from which they sprang.

We have much to learn from the Eastern religions, and we have much too to give them; but we are always in danger of forgetting the art of giving—of giving without strings—as Christ gave his life that all men might be made whole and integrated in the Church as she will surely be at the end of time—the Holy Catholic Church at last *de facto*, "in very fact", and not just *de jure*, "by legal right".

We must never forget the sufferings that the Church has from time to time inflicted on sincere men who could not see in her the true Church of Christ because she herself had marred the image; and, just as Gandhi saw in untouchability an "ineffaceable blot" and a "curse" that had fallen on Hinduism, so must we see that persecution, forced conversions, the burning of heretics, and all the other crimes that have been perpetrated in the name of Christ are an "ineffaceable blot" and a "curse" for which penance is still due. In the scale of time as evolution sees it, however, two thousand years is but a day, and we can only hope that the Church, to which all the other religions, in the course of their evolution, draw ever nearer in spirit and in doctrine, will one day so have purified herself that she will be able to show forth Jesus

Christ not only as the true Messiah, but also as the true Krishna, and the true Bodhisattva who takes upon himself the burden of saving all sentient beings until the end of time.

Seen in this context the Catholic Church is the middle way between the quest for individual salvation so typical of India and the quest for the corporate harmony of a perfect society that was China's ideal; it is the middle way between the absolute transcendence of the Muslim God and the absolute immanence of the Hindu Absolute; for transcendent and immanent meet absolutely only in one place, in the God-man, Jesus Christ, who is both the Lord whom we serve and the Bread by which we live.

Few of us are mystics, and it is because the Catholic Church brings the surety of mystical union with the Incarnate God to ordinary men in the Blessed Sacrament of the altar that even ordinary men are enabled to taste, however faintly, of "what things God hath prepared for them that love him". In the Blessed Sacrament the breach between matter and spirit and the breach between God and man are for ever healed; and we can only look forward in faith, hope and charity to the day when all men will "as living stones [be] built up, a spiritual house, . . . acceptable to God by Jesus Christ" (1 Pet. 2. 5). And it will be not only *our* house but the house of all those who from all the religions of the world may one day see fit to pour their spiritual treasures into it. That is how we, as Catholics, should see it; for we cannot afford to shun or reject the graces and true insights it has pleased God to scatter throughout the non-Christian world. Should we do this, then we can be very certain that we too will be shunned and rejected—and rightly so, for we will have failed to obey the second great commandment: to love your neighbour as yourself.

Perhaps the dark night of the secular involvement of the Catholic Church is really drawing to its close. In any case we must fervently hope that the new spirit which Pope John XXIII infused into the Church will, under God and the wise guidance of the present Holy Father, Pope Paul VI, and his successors, continue to grow in holiness and grace and to bring in an ever more abundant harvest.

# SELECT BIBLIOGRAPHY

*In this series:* DRIOTON, Etienne, CONTENAU, Georges, and DUCHESNE-GUILLEMIN, J.: *Religions of the Ancient East*; GARDET, Louis: *Mohammedanism*; LEMAITRE, Solange: *Hinduism*.

ASHBY, Philip H.: *The Conflict of Religions*, New York, Scribner, 1955.

BRANDON, S. G. F.: *Man and his Destiny in the Great Religions*, Manchester Univ. Press, 1962.

CUTTAT, J. A.: *The Encounter of Faiths*, New York, Desclée, 1960.

ELIADE, Mircea: *Patterns in Comparative Religion*, London and New York, Sheed and Ward, 1958.

JAMES, E. O.: *History of Religions*, London, English Universities Press, and New York, Rinehart, 1955.

KITAGAWA, Joseph M.: *Religions of the East*, Philadelphia, Westminster, 1960.

KRAEMER, Hendrik: *World Cultures and World Religions*, London, Lutterworth, 1960.

VAN DER LEEUW, G.: *Religion in Essence and Manifestation*, London, Allen and Unwin, and New York, Macmillan, 1938.

NEILL, Stephen: *Christian Faith and other Faiths*, London and New York, Oxford Univ. Press, 1961.

OTTO, Rudolph: *The Idea of the Holy*, London and New York, Oxford Univ. Press, 1920.

PARRINDER, Geoffrey: *Comparative Religion*, London, Allen and Unwin, 1962.

RADHAKRISHNAN, S.: *Eastern Religions and Western Thought*, London and New York, Oxford Univ. Press, 1939.

WACH, Joachim: *The Comparative Study of Religions*, New York, Columbia Univ. Press, 1958.

ZAEHNER, R. C.: *The Concise Encyclopedia of Living Faiths*, London, Hutchinson, and New York, Hawthorn, 1959; *At Sundry Times*, London, Faber, 1958; *The Convergent Spirit*, London, Routledge, 1963 (American edn, *Matter and Spirit*, New York, Harpers, 1963).

# The Twentieth Century Encyclopedia
# of Catholicism

*The number of each volume indicates its place in
the over-all series and not the order of publication.*

# TWENTIETH CENTURY ENCYCLOPEDIA OF CATHOLICISM

*Titles are subject to change.*